RUSSIAN ETIQUETTE & ETHICS IN BUSINESS

Drew Wilson   Lloyd Donaldson

Printed on recyclable paper

NTC Business Books
a division of *NTC Publishing Group* • Lincolnwood, Illinois USA

Library of Congress Cataloging-in-Publication Data

Wilson, Drew.
    Russian etiquette & ethics in business / Drew Wilson, Lloyd
Donaldson.
        p.   cm.
    Includes index.
    ISBN 0-8442-4216-0 (alk. paper)
    1. Business etiquette--Russia (Federation) 2. Business ethics-
-Russia (Federation) 3. Industrial management--Russia (Federation)
4. National characteristics, Russian.   I. Donaldson, Lloyd.
II. Title.
HF5389.W56   1995
395'.52'0947--dc20   95-47053
                                                                  CIP

Published by NTC Business Books, a division of NTC Publishing Group.
4255 West Touhy Avenue, Lincolnwood (Chicago), Illinois 60646-1975, U.S.A.
© 1996 by Drew Wilson and Lloyd Donaldson.
Manufactured in the United States of America.

67890 VP 9 8 7 6 5 4 3 2 1

CONTENTS

ACKNOWLEDGMENTS

The authors would like to thank the following people who made significant contributions to the book: John Gallant, for the historical overview "Russia and Her Foreigners Throughout History"; Nathaniel Trumball, for the section on natural resources; Management at Tambrand's St. Petersburg; Jurgen Feldhof, Sociology professor at University of Bielefeld in Germany; Elena Shershneva; Sociology professor at the University of St. Petersburg; Andrei Minin, Michael Mondini, Nell Romanov and Richard Torrence for general information, and the many others who spent time talking to the authors.

INTRODUCTION

The Second World

Traveling to Russia? Forget about bringing blue jeans, cigarettes and toilet paper. Don't take food for the length of your stay, or even over-the-counter Western medicines. All those stories about shortages are passé. In fact, you won't need to bring anything except money and patience.

In December 1991, when leaders of the Union of Soviet Socialist Republics (USSR) met in Minsk, Byelorussia and formed a loose confederation of separate countries called the Commonwealth of Independent States (CIS), Russia's gates flew open. The USSR had disappeared, and foreign products, services, people and ideas began pouring into the country. Old systems started collapsing while glimmers of new systems began to appear, creating an atmosphere of bewildering but fertile chaos.

Colliding waves of change continue to batter Russia. The rouble's value steadily drops—diminishing the already meager wages of citizens—as prices rise. Massive factories often can't pay their employees and many face bankruptcy. Business laws are formed, stretched, broken and reformed. Taxes grow, layer, fragment and change monthly. Social systems, such as education, law enforcement, transport and health care are in a severe crisis. Wealth is being redistributed. Organized crime wields a growing influence. Running in tandem with these factors is a sweeping wave of development. Small businesses are springing up, and the infrastructure is slowly being upgraded. Millions of dollars in foreign investment have rolled in with world lending institutions having doled out large sums for development. It's a great time to do business.

The Market Beckons . . .

Russia's 150 million plus consumers make up a potential market roughly comparable to that of the United States or European Community. Opportunities for adventurous foreign businesspeople abound. Russia is a vast storehouse of raw materials such as wood, oil, metals, diamonds. The service sector is grossly underdeveloped. Engineers and scientists produce impressive results with unimpressive tools. The workforce boasts a 99 percent literacy rate and an infrastructure, albeit aging, is in place. Business does not need to be built from the ground up, but rather converted from a defense-based, state-run system to a more efficient, consumer-oriented one. *Conversion* has become a buzzword in Russia.

The vast majority of foreign businesses are only importing goods, but some companies like UK-based Tambrands and Coca-Cola already have manufacturing ventures up and running—erecting high entry barriers for competitors. Setting up shop now is twice as difficult and costly as it was only one year ago. Yet foreign businesses keep on coming despite start-up costs—and substantial risks.

Political infighting and widespread corruption continue to cripple free market reforms. In October 1993, President Yeltsin ordered tanks to blow away his opposition in Parliament, then demanded new elections across the country. But Russian nationalists and Communists still fill the Parliament and clamor for a rollback to strong centralized control. Other influential political groups want to slow the pace of reform to cushion the blow for Russians suffering from tight monetary policies. Key reformers have either resigned or been pushed out. Palace intrigue prevails and rumors flame through the media almost daily. Where Russia is headed, nobody really knows. Foreign businesspeople have described today's Russia variously as "The Wild West," as "A buried treasure that reveals only a small jewel in the sand" and as "A giant casino where they keep changing the rules."

It's easy to criticize Russia. Her brilliant scientists created the world's only orbiting space station but the antennas on top rickety electric buses often pop off the overhead wire track, forcing the driver to climb on the bus roof and reattach them.

Visitors will find countless other examples. There will be recurring inconveniences; poor customer service; illogical, terrible waste; and shameless corruption. Resist giving unsolicited advice and instruction. Russians know things are bad—and they're trying to cope. Russians are also a particularly proud people, highly sensitive to outsiders' critical opinions and instruction. It's unbearable for them to watch foreign businesspeople arrive believing they are emissaries of light, bringing modern ideas to the natives living in the dark forest.

Bear in mind that the average Russian holds a deep sense of humiliation and fear. During Soviet times, the USSR was a world superpower, keeping the United States in check. Russians lived under a rigid and predictable system that laid out requirements for each citizen in every stage of life. It was the person's duty to follow, and obedience meant certain guarantees such as free education, life-long employment and a comfortable standard of living. The family was cared for by the system and life was relatively simple.

Post-Soviet Russia didn't emerge but rather exploded into the world—spreading a sentiment of cynicism. Russians fondly remember the halcyon past—which means just five years ago. To plunge from security into confusion and despair so fast and to face an uncertain future destroys some people and torments others.

Russians have a history of blaming outsiders for their troubles. Foreign companies are viewed as wealthy businesses that offer a secure place to work. But, those which establish themselves without thoughtful consideration for the Russian way are viewed as invaders.

But Meet Russia Halfway or Fail

Foreign business success stories share a common ingredient— the willingness to learn about the Russian way and adopt parts of their operation to it. A joint venture involves both teaching and learning. Grand failures result when a foreign company insists on rigid adherence to the Western way. Many foreign businesspeople come to Russia expecting that rational, efficient and orderly management alone will overcome cultural difficulties and get production rolling—they couldn't be more wrong. As some companies have found out the hard way, mighty Russia is not for the naive, weak or impatient.

To succeed in Russia, the first step is trying to understand Russians. But Russians defy easy categorization. A common mistake is assuming they are European, which they are not. The Renaissance and the Reformation barely touched their ancestors. Russia is neither European nor Asian, not First World and not Third World. The truth lies somewhere in between, in the Second World.

1

THE RUSSIAN
EMPIRE

Russia and Her Foreigners
Throughout History

Russia's history is long, and mostly tragic. Russians have suffered at the hands of invaders, and they have suffered at the hands of their own rulers. Its people take pride in their ability to weather adversity, and, on the whole, Russians know more about their history than Americans know about theirs. What's more, Russians enjoy telling others about their motherland's many sacrifices.

Not even the deepest understanding of Russian history will enable foreign entrepreneurs to cut through bureaucratic red tape, fathom unclear and constantly changing legislation, or understand what's going on behind the eyes of their Russian partners. However, knowing some history can provide some perspective—Russians have never made it easy for foreigners in their country. Also, a foreigner showing some familiarity with Russian history and culture will make a good impression on Russians.

Two threads run through Russian history: (1) the competition between Westerners and Slavophiles, and (2) Russians' perception of foreigners. With regard to the first, there have been two schools of thought on how Russia should best fulfill its potential. They are: should it emulate the West by absorbing the knowledge and technology of foreigners, or should it build a society based on its own religious and cultural heritage? Westernizers advocated the first course, and favored Russia's development of science, trade, and technology. The late Andrei Sakharov, father of Russia's atomic bomb and an ardent democrat, would be considered a Westernizer. Slavophiles tended to be more old-fashioned and religious, finding virtue in the life of the peasant. Leo Tolstoy and Aleksander Solzhenitsyn are two well-known authors who fall into this category.

With regard to the second thread, Russians have traditionally mistrusted foreigners. Even in the seventeenth century, foreign businessmen, craftsmen, and military advisors in Russia lived in walled-off compounds inaccessible to ordinary Russian citizens. Foreigners did not belong to the Russian Orthodox church, and were, therefore, considered heretics. When orthodox Marxism-Leninism replaced Orthodox Christianity, foreigners were again stigmatized for not having the correct beliefs. Long ago, Russians used the word now applied to Germans (*nemets*) to refer to all foreigners. *Nemets* is related to the Russian word for "dumb," *nemoi*. The word *Slav* is connected to the Russian word *slovo*, or "word." Russians believed they alone were endowed with the gift of speech and outsiders were not. Russians today refer to their guests as *inostrantsy*, or people from other countries.

Anybody familiar with contemporary Russia will see similarities between the treatment foreigners received earlier in Russian history and that they receive today. Russian goals in their dealings with foreigners have also changed little over the years. While there is more interest in acquiring consumer goods and services in Russia now than in the past, the main objectives are the same as they have been for three centuries—technological and commercial parity with the West. As for the foreigners to the East, Russians have never held these eastern neighbors in high regard. This is in large part a result of the treatment they received at the hands of the Mongols.

Beginnings of the Russian State

Rurik, a ninth-century conqueror from Scandinavia, and his descendants made Kiev the main city of the earliest Russian state. By the twelfth century, Orthodox Christianity had come to Russia through Kiev, as had many artistic, architectural, and literary traditions. In 1240, Mongol armies from the East sacked Kiev. At its height, the Mongol empire included most of present-day Russia. For some 200 years, Mongol khans imposed heavy taxes on their Russian subjects. Any attempt to refuse payment was met with brutal punishment. In one famous case, a group of uncooperative Russian nobles was assembled and forced to lie face down on the ground. A heavy wooden gate was thrown on top of them, and several Mongol soldiers set up a table and chairs on the top side of the gate. A banquet lasting several hours followed, during which the Russian resistors were crushed to death as the soldiers ate and drank their fill. Such demonstrations were put on from time to time to show what could happen to others who tried to resist.

Bloody and burdensome as the Mongol period was, the Mongols introduced many administrative and military concepts to Russia. Many contemporary Russian words have their roots in the Mongol language. *Kreml* (Kremlin), *dyengi* (money), and *chin* (rank) are three words that today are very much a part of any Russian's vocabulary. Many historians feel that the most enduring legacy of the Mongol period is the fact that Russia was isolated from Europe during the European Renaissance. This, they say, led to a national inferiority complex and a tendency to look inward for solutions to national problems. While this is certainly true, another factor that made Russia inward-looking was the establishment of Moscow as the "third Rome" of Christianity. In 989, Duke Vladimir I adopted Orthodox Christianity as his religion and that of Russia. Later, during the ascendancy of Moscow, Russia's church split from that in Constantinople.

This freed Russians from the need for spiritual guidance from outside Russia, and allowed later czars to appoint patriarchs whose views were compatible with their own. Though the Mongols imposed a heavy economic burden on the Russian people, political and cultural interference was less severe. The church was exempt from taxes, and the Mongols allowed Russian princes to administer small geographical areas. As long as the princes paid taxes to their Mongol masters, they were free to rule their areas as they liked.

During the thirteenth, fourteenth, and fifteenth centuries the rulers of the area that included Moscow became the strongest in Russia. As the Mongol empire grew weaker and the Moscow princes increased their power and absorbed other princedoms, Russia became harder for the Mongols to govern. Dmitri Donskoi, a Moscow prince, dealt the Mongols their first military defeat in Russia in 1380 in the famous Battle of Kulikovo. It was not until a century later, though, that Ivan III became the first Russian prince to refuse with impunity to pay tribute to the Mongols.

For over three centuries the focus of Russia's affairs with non-Russian peoples was to the south and east of Russia. Only when the Mongols had been defeated could Moscow, by then the premier principality in Russia, turn its eyes to the West. Russia's reorientation toward the West did not happen right away. Ivan IV (1530–84), the grandson of Ivan III, reinforced Moscow's preeminence in Russia by conquering lands the Mongols left behind as they retreated to the east. This done, Ivan IV went to war with his neighbors to the west. In a war that lasted from 1558 to 1583 and set Russia without success against the empires of Poland/Lithuania and Sweden, Ivan exacted tributes from the Russian people that were every bit as harsh as those imposed by the Mongols.

Ivan IV's cruel authoritarianism earned him the nickname Ivan the Terrible (*Ivan Grozny*). It is interesting to note that *grozny* does not mean what most speakers of English mean when they say "terrible" (i.e., "He is a terrible bridge player"). It means "capable of unleashing great terror." It is also interesting that Stalin was a great admirer of Ivan IV. It was during Stalin's time that the epic Soviet film biography of Ivan IV was produced; Ivan is portrayed as the kind of leader Russia needed in difficult times—cruel and harsh, yet strong enough to do what was necessary for the good of Russia.

Rise of the Romanovs

Ivan IV was married seven times and had four sons. The first son, Dimitri, died as an infant. Ivan killed his second son, who would have been Ivan V if he had survived, with a metal-tipped staff in a fit of anger. The third son, Fyodor, became czar in 1584. But Fyodor's strength of character was no match for that of his wife's brother, Boris Godunov. It was Boris Godunov who ruled Russia while Fyodor was czar; he then became czar himself when Fyodor died without leaving a male heir. Many scholars hold that Boris Godunov had Ivan IV's youngest son, named Dimitri, murdered.

A 29-year period of political murders, intrigue, and foreign invasions followed. Finally, in 1613, the council of Russian nobles elected Ivan IV's grandnephew czar to put an end to what has become known as "the time of troubles." The grandnephew, Michael Romanov (1598–1645), was the first of the Romanov dynasty, which would rule Russia until 1917.

Turning Toward Europe

Over the next hundred years Russia made its first steps toward contact with Europe. Trade with England and Holland began, as did diplomatic exchanges. Better educated Russians learned Latin, Greek, and Polish. The major objective of these contacts was to acquire knowledge and technology that would increase Russia's military strength.

It was Peter I, also known as Peter the Great (1672–1725), who fervently believed that Russia must enter the European world of commerce and diplomacy in order to become a great nation. When he was eleven years old, Peter saw the *streltsy*, or palace guard, rampage through the Kremlin. The guards brutally killed several resident statesmen and nobles on the strength of a politically inspired rumor. One group of *streltsy* would chase down its victims and toss them over the side of a high staircase inside the Kremlin, while on the floor below the staircase stood another group of *streltsy* with upturned spears. The spectacle left Peter with a desire to leave Moscow and its institutions behind and create something better some-where else.

As he grew older, Peter began spending time with Western businessmen and military advisors, who lived in a walled-off suburb of Moscow reserved for foreigners. Ordinary Russians did not enter the foreigners' compound, but, as czar, Peter could come and go as he pleased. Peter learned soldiering from a Scottish military adviser; shipbuilding from Dutch boat-builders; and blacksmithing from English craftsmen. His was the hand that created Russia's first navy, and it was he who saw that, in order to enter the world of European commerce, he would also need a large commercial fleet. Peter instituted a number of radical reforms, including the complete reorganization of the state's administration, the revamping of the military along Western lines, and the placing of the church under direct state control.

The reforms were fiercely resisted in Russia. For ordinary Russians, it was enough to know that God was benevolent, the czar was healthy, and the old ways would continue. They were not interested in reform. Even Russia's more worldly citizens, nobles who sported the latest fashions from Poland, considered many of Peter's ideas outlandish. Peter was called, among other things, a heretic and an antichrist.

In 1703 construction of the city of St. Petersburg began. The peasantry was subjected to compulsory labor for this immense project, and those who had property paid heavy taxes. St. Petersburg became the new capital of Russia—the culmination of Peter's desire to rid Russia of its inward, Moscow-based worldview and replace it with one oriented to the West.

During the reign of Peter the Great, foreign know-how and technology were prized. Despite the distaste most Russians felt for the heathen foreigners, the Russian government offered foreign engineers, craftsmen, military advisors and others good salaries and the opportunity to pass their knowledge on to eager apprentices. Peter wanted Russia to participate in the commercial, diplomatic and military affairs of Europe. Learning the ways of the West was, in his view, the best way to accomplish this goal.

During this period many new words entered the Russian language. The story of *zont*, the Russian word for umbrella, is a particularly interesting example. The Dutch word for umbrella is *zondek*, which Russians pronounced *zontik*. Since *-ik* is a removable suffix Russians add to words to convey smallness or cuteness, the *-ik* is sometimes left off, leaving *zont*.

Through the eighteenth and nineteenth centuries, Russia's role in European affairs grew. Russian iron and lumber industries developed along Western lines, and its army, also increasingly modeled along European lines, enabled Russian rulers to expand their territory. Of course, as Russia's military strength increased, so did Russia's participation in the European diplomatic theater. During these times Western businessmen and advisors came to Russia in increasing numbers. Russia also sent some of its most promising young people abroad to learn Western ways and bring back their knowledge to serve their country. A third point of contact with the West was wealthy Russians traveling to Europe for amusement. By the nineteenth century, French was used more than Russian in many upper-class households. Some works of Leo Tolstoy contain French phrases in settings where members of the nobility are engaged in conversation.

Exposure to Westerners, however, did more for Russia than help it modernize its army and develop its industry. As Russians learned to read French, English, and German, they gained access to the ideas of Rousseau, John Locke, and Karl Marx. In parlors at soirees in Moscow and St. Petersburg members of what became known as the *intelligentsiya* discussed such issues as the need for creative freedom in Russia and the moral evils of serfdom.

The Great Experiment

As the nineteenth century came to a close, conditions for the rank and file in Russia grew increasingly dismal. Groups of reformers and revolutionaries formulated their programs of action on the basis of the ideas brought to Russia and discussed by the *intelligentsiya*. Some of these groups were Western-oriented. They advocated intellectual debate and cultural expression found in Western-style democracies. Groups with a Slavophile outlook advocated traditional agriculturally based Russian social and political programs.

At that time, Bolshevik ideology contained elements of both Western and Slavophile programs. Internationalism and a focus on the urban worker were Western ideas, yet the ideas of withdrawing from World War I and handing over farmland to the peasants also gave the Bolshevik platform a Slavophile flavor.

While urban Russians had a certain understanding of the Bolshevik program, the peasantry was not so well informed. Sometimes this worked to the Bolsheviks' advantage. A case in point involves the Bolshevik goal of providing electric power to rural Russia. The Russian word for electricity is *elektrifikatsiya*. The syllable *lek* sounds like *lik*, which in Russian connotes faces in religious icons. Peasants, who did not know what electricity was, assumed that the Bolsheviks were in favor of religious icons. In this way Lenin and his comrades won some unanticipated support in the countryside.

During the period preceding the Revolution, foreigners might have been considered a necessary economic presence, greedy capitalists whose sole interest was to enrich themselves at the expense of Russia, or welcome fellow revolutionaries. Those at the left end of the political spectrum looked with favor on Westerners; after all, like-minded Germans, Englishmen, and others were valuable allies who would foment revolutions in their countries. Groups that advocated the cause of rural Russians looked less favorably on Westerners, their wars, and the world economy.

Stalin (1879–1953) has been described by Western scholars as paranoid, messianic, ruthless and absolutely tyrannical. Many Russians today would say that this description barely scratches the surface, while others in Russia say that, though Stalin was strict and there may have been oppression, people had jobs and crime was rare.

Many hallmarks of Soviet politics, society and economy were established under Stalin: collectivized agriculture, an inflexible centrally planned economy, censorship in the press and arts and the pervasive role of the Communist Party in all these areas are some of the major ones. Foreigners were wanted for their technical expertise and nothing else. During the reign of Peter the Great, it was foreigners' nonadherence to Russian religion that made them distasteful; now it was their nonbelief in Marxism-Leninism. News and ideas from outside the USSR were kept out, and news about the Soviet Union reported to the outside world was closely monitored. Unfriendly journalists were not welcome.

Stalin's objectives were narrower than those of Peter the Great. Both leaders were eager to strengthen their armies. Unlike Stalin however, Peter saw contact with Westerners as beneficial. Peter sought out knowledgeable people from other countries in order to learn how to make Russia better. Stalin vilified everything foreign and perpetuated the myth that the achievements of the Soviet Union surpassed those of other countries.

Though Stalinist ideology was quasireligious in its portrayal of Moscow as the source of world salvation, one could not call Stalin a Slavophile. He reduced the status of the church to that of a minor industrial ministry while turning most churches into museums. His programs of forced collectivization, grain confiscation, and resettlement of large numbers of peasants can hardly be said to have benefited the peasantry. His violence, cruelty and repression turned Russia into an immense prison camp. The USSR's unnaturally rapid industrialization under Stalin did amount to a Westward push. Stalin's policies, however, resulted in the deaths of tens of millions of Soviet citizens from high party functionaries and senior military officers to ordinary clerks, workers, and farmers.

The fear and suspicion of foreigners generated under Stalin did not evaporate under Khrushchev, Brezhnev and Gorbachev. During the Cold War, espionage was practiced by the Soviets, Americans and many others. In the USSR, the spy game had as its object the capture of information and technology that would help the Soviet Union achieve military and economic parity with the West. These goals were the same as those of Peter the Great; however, the rules and methods had changed dramatically in the intervening 250 years.

Post Communism

Russia's rejection of communism in 1990, when the Communist Party gave up its monopoly on power, generated a wide variety of opinions from Western Russia-watchers and a new crop of Russian commentators offering their opinions in the Western media. Some claimed that, with the cumbersome ideology of communism in the rubbish heap, Russia was finally poised to unleash its huge economic and cultural potential under a free market democracy. Others cautioned that Russians, unaccustomed to the risks and rewards of Western-style economic and political systems, would go through a long period of hardship and instability before their lives began to improve.

With its abundant natural resources, large potential markets, and many well-trained and highly competent scientists and engineers, Russia offers opportunities to the right investors. However, the legacy of eight decades of communism includes many things to frighten potential businesspeople. An inadequate infrastructure, outmoded industrial technology, and a poorly trained workforce only top a long list. Add to this ecological catastrophes and the pervasive crime and political instability that are reported daily in the newspapers, and doing business in Russia looks even more risky.

Those who do choose to trade with Russians are the newest generation of players in a game that began over 300 years ago. Just as their predecessors did, they bring with them new technology, and new work and management styles. The words they are adding to the Russian language today include "spreadsheet" and "voucher." Many find Russians more interested in acquiring technology than becoming familiar with the ideas associated with that technology. Often they find themselves mistrusted by their Russian partners. The military advisors and businessmen who came to Russia in the seventeenth and eighteenth centuries received similar treatment. As did those who followed them during the time of the czars and the Bolsheviks. Two things that they all have had in common are a taste for adversity and a spirit of adventure.

2
THE SOVIET SYSTEM

The Soviet Imprint

The Union of Soviet Socialist Republics was created by the Bolsheviks in 1922 after the Revolution. Russia was transformed from an autocracy ruled by czars into a totalitarian state ruled by the Communist Party. Josef Stalin, the brutal dictator of the USSR, forced the pace of modernization at enormous human and environmental cost. The USSR expanded its territory and sphere of influence during and after World War II by forcibly incorporating areas such as the Baltic States and Moldavia and taking firm control of most of Eastern Europe. It continued a policy of expansion nearly up to its demise in 1991.

Concepts that characterized the Soviet state included power, invincibility, seriousness and triumph. Sensitivity, compassion and humor were virtually outlawed. Soviet art, particularly paintings and sculptures, reflected the philosophy; clear and conservative ideas over imaginative ones, strength and girth over detail and flexibility, flaming or dark colors over cool or varied hues.

Physical labor was the Soviet citizen's purpose and through honest communal endeavors, serving the communist cause, the Soviet citizen would build a new world, a communist paradise that promised a future blissful life and untold riches. Through his unwavering discipline and iron will, the new socialist man would lead the world to this paradise. Women were viewed as strong, athletic, capable of doing their share, but always a step behind the man.

Many Russians will claim that few fundamental divisions exist between a Soviet person and a Russian. However, usually they agree to one main difference: the Russian person has his own opinion; the Soviet person was not allowed to.

The Facade

During the Moscow Olympics in 1980, key parts of the city were freshly painted, roads were resurfaced, and shops were filled with imported goods. Alcoholics were gathered up and bused to the suburbs. These tidying up measures were undertaken to impress foreigners visiting the Games. When the Olympics ended, Moscow returned to its former self, the imported goods were removed from the shops, alcoholics were brought back to their homes and buildings were left to soil and deteriorate. Such deception, involving cosmetic as opposed to substantial change, is known as *pokhazuhka* (for show) and was a practice central to the Soviet system.

Pokhazuhka can be traced back to the legendary "Potemkin Village" incident. In the nineteenth century, when Catherine the Great wanted to tour by boat the land she ruled along the Dnieper River, Count Potemkin, an influential industrialist, ordered facades of buildings and shops be erected on the river banks, giving the appearance of prosperous communities, when indeed, behind the facades were wilderness. The phrase *Potemkin Village* became to be known as a synonym for deception.

Cultivating Resources

Russia has never developed a layer of small producers and craftsmen, or a society that was capable of internally resolving economic problems, according to Alexander Akhiyezer of Russia's Institute of Economic Forecasting.

Akhiyezer argues Russia has developed a "culture of poverty" in which it solves economic problems by exploiting more and more of its vast resources instead of increasing returns from existing ones. He traces the practice back to early Russian agriculturists who, constrained by a short growing season, increased production by extensive methods—cultivating more of the seemingly endless land—rather than by intensive methods, such as making more effective use of existing land.

When Russia began to industrialize it followed the same pattern, pulling in resources—in this case ideas, technology and finance—from the West. Peter the Great focused extensively on creating major enterprises including mines, weapons plants and foundries. According to Akhiyezer, that focus retarded the development of a free market and individual entrepreneurs. By the end of the nineteenth century, labor was overwhelmingly concentrated in major enterprises which the Soviet system took over, replacing a thin layer of rich industrialists with a single rich figure—the state.

A curious footnote took place at the end of the 1920s, after Stalin's ruthless and brutal collectivization of farms. Russian farmers were allowed to retain their own small plots of land. These private little strips covered barely 5 percent of arable land—and yielded 25 percent of gross agricultural output!

Akhiyezer argues that Russia is at a turning point where it must rid itself of the belief that it can simply continue to consume resources.

The Work Ethic

The Soviet government instilled in people the idea that everything was free—all benefits were guaranteed—thus, severely distorting the concept of the value of work. Soviets lacked the inner growth and understanding which comes through the process of investigation, conception and production. Moreover, young persons were often discouraged from working as stories of capitalist exploitation of child laborers were a part of government propaganda.

Nobody was taught how to work for themselves. Soviet ideology professed that a man working for himself was an egoist, a disgrace, someone who can't live in society. A good Soviet meant working for others, for communism. Money was the last item on a Soviet citizen's priority list.

Ecological Nightmares

The communist doctrine stressed industrialization. Nature was to be harnessed and used for the prosperity of the state and the people. Massive dams were flung across mighty rivers for power generation in complete disregard of possible ecological damage. Huge factory complexes mushroomed across the country as the result of the government's five-year plans. Lakes and streams became heavily polluted from uncontrolled chemical dumping. (In one case, phenol accidentally came through the kitchen faucets of an entire city.) Unchecked factory emissions poisoned the air. Radioactive materials were stored within meters of residential areas; nuclear waste was dumped in Russia's northern seas and occasionally launched into orbit around the earth.

There were no environmental movements—no public outcries. Ruthless, virtually unregulated industrial expansion was rooted in patriotism, necessary to grow the great Soviet state. The resulting large-scale ecological destruction will hurt Russia for a long time.

The near-meltdown into the water table of the Chernobyl Nuclear Power Plant in 1986 was merely one of many environmental catastrophes in the former USSR. Chernobyl elicited international panic after a monitoring team in Sweden one day detected unusual amounts of radiation in the air. Gorbachev, despite his passionate drive for openness in the USSR, refused to admit the extent of the accident until foreign pressure for an explanation mounted. Other Soviet ecological nightmares, however, were easier to conceal.

One showpiece of the Soviet regime was the introduction of cotton to the desert of the Central Asian Republics. The new cotton crop, now flourishing in what was once a parched desert, was proudly featured in books and films as a miracle of Soviet technology. But cotton grew in the desert only at the expense of the Aral Sea. Cotton plants demanded huge amounts of water. The extensive irrigation systems that were dug drew too much water from the seemingly inexhaustible Amurdarya River and others like it that fed the Aral Sea. As a result, the Aral started to evaporate, ruining the region's delicate environmental balance.

Today, former port cities are miles from the shrinking sea. The sea's edges are strewn with beached ships. The contracting sea is becoming more saline.

For years the area was off-limits to foreigners as Soviet experts grappled with the problem. When a solution was found, it was on a scale as lofty as the scheme that initially caused the chaos. Scientists suggested a multibillion dollar diversion of northern Siberian rivers to the South in order to fill the dying sea. But nothing was done and locals started to joke, and still do, that if every expert who came to the Aral Sea to study it brought a bucket of water the problem would be solved in no time. With the breakup of the Soviet Union, responsibility falls to the region's new states.

Ecology is not considered a pressing issue in Russia. On a governmental level environmental legislation carries little value. The Green Movement is tiny, political lobbying is in its infancy, and the population remains largely ignorant of environmental issues. Groups of Russians will trek through a forest or park, blithely leaving trash in their wake.

It is not just clean-ups that are at issue. Environmental issues have not been effectively integrated into industrial and city planning. Safety standards can be low. Chernobyl's reactors, and others like them built in Russia, lack the extra protective shielding mandatory in many foreign countries. On a more basic level, inefficient and polluting landfill techniques still dominate trash disposal. Russia's second largest city, St. Petersburg, with a population of five million that generates thousands of tons of garbage a day, has no compacting or baling plants to compress trash, or any other high technology equipment to deal with it.

The vastness of the country and the state's control of the media have helped conceal disasters in the past. Today most people are more preoccupied with surviving day to day than worrying about an oil spill a thousand miles away, however devastating the damage may be.

3

THE COLLAPSE OF THE USSR

Managing the Decline of an Empire

In the late 1970s, a pregnant Soviet woman likely brought costly gifts to an acquaintance at a hospital who would see to it that a specific doctor, with an esteemed reputation, delivered her baby. If a man wanted to buy a car it entailed a two-year wait—unless he delivered presents to a friend of a friend at an auto factory. Whether buying choice cuts of beef or hiring a plumber, applying for an apartment or getting a job promotion, Soviets knew connections and bribes were a part of life.

Not only were the everyday nuts and bolts of the immense Soviet machine showing corrosion, the core engine in Moscow sputtered and groaned, and the navigation system was broken. Corruption and inefficiency flourished within the ruling elite at all levels, from the state factory to the Kremlin. A spare tractor part that was needed in Poland first had to be requisitioned through Moscow, and the delay could shut down an entire farm. Production in antiquated factories was falling; shortages and shoddy workmanship were typical. Monstrous bureaucracies ensured economic mismanagement.

On the social level, alcoholism was rising and life expectancy was falling. Motivation, creativity and innovation were punished; mass obedience and passivity had been instilled. Few people believed in the promise of a future communist paradise where all would be equal and work was unnecessary, and communist rhetoric was seen as a cynical joke among the majority. Still, a pleasing stability reigned: Life was generously subsidized and nearly everybody was in the same boat.

The towering problems were masked by official rhetoric emphasizing grand achievements. Failures and corruption were concealed and tolerated. Instead, comfortably entrenched party officials devoted their energy to internal power plays. Criticizing the system brought severe punishment from the state.

Such was the climate during the time of Leonid Brezhnev, the conservative General Secretary of the Communist Party, who disliked change and maneuvered to preserve the USSR's stagnation. Meanwhile, the West was making dramatic advances in many fields, particularly telecommunications, microelectronics and industrial modernization, thereby, widening the economic gap between the two superpowers.

When Brezhnev died in 1982, Yuri Andropov, an aging ex-KGB chief, assumed the helm. Andropov was actually the first Soviet leader to start the move toward market socialism. Andropov began a critical questioning of the USSR's condition—the first Soviet leader to speak the truth openly. He believed in a more open society with a vibrant civilian economy, rather than escalating investment in the bloated military-industrial complex. Such ideas were dangerous at the time, but nobody wanted to point that out to a former longstanding KGB chief.

Andropov brought to Moscow like-minded men who understood the need for reforms and advanced fresh ideas. One such person was Mikhail Gorbachev, who became the leader's protégé. Andropov died in February 1984 and Konstantin Chernenko, an ancient Communist Party figure, took over as leader. As a staunch conservative, Chernenko favored the stagnation of the Brezhnev era, muffling cries for change. Chernenko's reign only lasted about one year. When he passed away in March 1985, a relatively youthful and energetic Mikhail Gorbachev was elected General Secretary of the Communist Party.

For a Soviet leader, Gorbachev was strikingly different. He was in his early fifties while most of the high party officials were more than two decades older. He had radical new ideas; a burning desire for change; a preference for reason and facts instead of rhetoric; and a seemingly boundless optimism.

The new leader believed Soviets had been conditioned into a passive and unthinking mass dependent on the government for all, and that this threatened the USSR's longevity. He felt that radical changes in government and society were needed.

His plan was a restructuring (*perestroika*) of Soviet society and he wasted no time. He dislodged many Brezhnevite bureaucrats and incompetent party members, installing instead so-called new thinkers who shared his reform ideas. He hammered at the party elite, who would suffer in silent resentment when he cut off their dogmatic moralizing and demanded instead a practical plan of action.

Gorbachev believed in communism, but no longer in fomenting worldwide workers' revolutions; he believed in a strong military, but no longer in solving all problems through warfare. He was the first Russian reformer to attempt fundamental changes without violence, terror and deception. He believed the challenge was from within the Soviet people; outsiders were not to blame. A populist in the true sense, he typically went to common people, unannounced, and asked for input into political change.

Having spent most of his political career in provincial Stavropol, Gorbachev lacked the high-level political experience and *svyazi* (connections) necessary for pushing through his reforms. His radical proposals threatened the power base of the ruling elite and his insistence on defense cuts angered the powerful Soviet military. Hard-line party officials made up the majority and they wouldn't budge. To break the deadlock and energize *perestroika*, Gorbachev initiated support from the public through *glasnost* (openness in society).

Through *glasnost*, Gorbachev saw a way to revive people from mental sloth and apathy. If the media were given freer reign to expose corruption and incompetence, the indignant public would be roused to civic action, he reasoned. *Glasnost*, which dissolved decades of ironclad censorship, uncorked what had been bottled up. Lively public debate filled the newspapers. Banned movies and books were allowed to circulate. Official history was questioned. Newspapers and television detailed outrageous corruption. Incompetent officials were uncovered and pushed out. Decadent privileges of the *nomenklatura* (the highest level social group) were exposed.

Emerging as a populist anticorruption fighter was a party official from Sverdlovsk, Boris Yeltsin, brought to Moscow by Gorbachev. Yeltsin began making a name for himself in Moscow by championing the common man and demanding answers to hardships in Soviet life such as waiting in lengthy lines or facing food shortages.

Relishing their new freedoms was a potentially powerful social force, the *intelligentsiya*, which was the impetus behind the Bolshevik Revolution. Gorbachev knew that these writers, artists, professors, musicians and scientists were vital to the success of his reforms. When Gorbachev later freed political dissidents, the *intelligentsiya* rallied around his leadership and *perestroika*.

Glasnost initially had a real impact on a jaded, resigned public. Yet, for the average Soviet citizen, nothing changed. In fact, things began to get worse—significant economic reforms had been delayed, half implemented or obstructed by the Old Guard. Reforms that had been implemented confused the public. Factories allowed to run without Moscow's control didn't know how to proceed without guidance and workers in a new pay system which linked productivity to wages were angry when they received lower salaries. No managerial class was under development and no technical assistance had been coordinated for industrial modernization. *Glasnost* made for engrossing reading, but did not put consumer goods into the stores. *Perestroika* became the butt of jokes.

Yet Gorbachev had to push forward. U.S. technological advances threatened the USSR in its weakened state. Soviet industry hadn't changed since the late 1950s. The Kremlin ignored advances in microelectronics while the rest of the world raced to computerize. Gorbachev was especially fearful of the Strategic Defense Initiative (SDI) promoted by Ronald Reagan, which threatened to give the U.S. military superiority in outer space. At nuclear arms summits he haggled with Reagan in futile attempts to slow the development of SDI. But, a Western military threat wasn't his pressing concern; the economic threat was. Gorbachev believed that his empire's deterioration and the West's prosperity would sink the USSR closer to Third World status.

All along, Gorbachev had been courting Europe, hoping it would be a fountain of financial and technical aid for Soviet modernization. But to woo Europe, military threats had to be diluted. In 1988, he began withdrawing troops from Afghanistan and reduced involvement in Kampuchea and Angola. He welcomed meetings with European leaders and offered sweeping arms cuts. He prodded Eastern European countries toward the direction of Russia's reform, promising Soviet military assistance only to those satellites instituting real change.

Meanwhile, staggering costs of the Chernobyl nuclear plant disaster, the Afghan war, the Armenian earthquake and a huge budget deficit piled up. Releasing Eastern Europe was one way to redirect sorely needed money and energy, and to pull in generous international aid that might help save *perestroika*.

Eastern Europe's subsequent turmoil would then be the burden of the West: floods of refugees, dangerous nationalism, the alarming costs of budget deficits, reunification and modernization. When Poland, Czechoslovakia and Hungary began testing the limits of freedom, Moscow didn't intervene. One by one the Soviet satellite countries, for decades forcibly held in Moscow's grip, declared independence without penalty. In November 1989, the Berlin Wall came down, effectively ending the Cold War.

Soon Lithuania, buoyed by liberated Eastern Europe, declared but did not get independence. Estonia and Latvia followed, unleashing strong anti-Russian sentiment. The southern republics and even Ukraine were soon demanding their independence. Gorbachev, under pressure from conservatives and sensing the imminent catastrophic collapse of the empire, sent troops into Lithuania to restore order. A military solution proved disastrous and by 1991 the Baltic States had broken free of Moscow's grip.

On the home front, *perestroika* hadn't moved from talk to action. Growing anticommunist sentiment threatened the nature of the system itself and Gorbachev sensed it. In February 1990, he asked the Communist Party to give up its constitutionally guaranteed monopoly on power, a monumental act dismantling the communist system. The party complied and, for the first time in Russian history, the ruling elite had to compete for power through a democratic process.

Communism was gone, the Soviet empire breaking up and *perestroika* dead. Organized crime thrived amid the chaos. The economy was in a state of emergency, factories couldn't pay employees, many shops were empty and available food was hoarded. Famine was also possible. Diamonds and gold were sold cheap on the world market to buy imported food. Gorbachev asked for and received foreign aid.

When Gorbachev vacationed at his *dacha* in the south of Russia in late August 1991, conservative hard liners staged a coup, seizing power in the name of the Communist Party. Gorbachev was detained at his summer home, while troops and tanks filled Moscow's streets to back up the coup plotters. But amid the chaos, Boris Yeltsin dramatically stood atop a tank, declared the coup illegal and, through his strong public support, assumed control of the nation. Later, when Gorbachev returned to Moscow, Yeltsin publicly chastised him for neglect and inaction, which had allowed the country to slip to a dangerous level. Gorbachev initially challenged Yeltsin's claim to power but soon left Moscow in defeat.

In December 1991, Yeltsin and the leaders of the Soviet republics met in Minsk, Byelorussia. To the surprise of the entire world, and even to Kremlin insiders, the leaders agreed to dismantle the Soviet Union and replace it with a loose confederation of states known as the Commonwealth of Independent States (CIS).

Today opinion is highly polarized. The vast majority of Russians hold a strong dislike, bordering on hatred, for Gorbachev. They blame him for Russia's current crisis, convinced he ruined the empire with his careless economic and social experiments because he was more concerned about his place in history. He pledged change but nothing changed. In trying to please both reformers and conservatives, he diluted his initial reform plans and brought ruin instead. Many Russians believe the August 1991 coup was staged to bring Gorbachev sympathy and allow him a relatively graceful exit.

Yet in the West, Gorbachev enjoys high respect as one of the most influential historical figures of the twentieth century.

He ended the Cold War, reduced the chances of worldwide nuclear destruction and managed the collapse of the vast Soviet empire without bloody revolution.

The Fall of the Soviet Economy

Soviet defense spending was large, but not large enough to topple the economy. Operating expenses of the world's largest welfare state, a series of natural disasters and a growing budget deficit added up, but were not at the root of economic decay. What was fundamentally wrong with the Soviet economy? The centrally planned economy was tightly controlled by the huge Moscow bureaucracy and was inadequately designed to encourage leading edge innovation and continually improve itself. More specifically, economists at the World Bank in Washington, D.C. speculate that the Soviets' inability to give workers an increasingly efficient means of production was the driving force behind the steady economic decline.

Recovering from the devastation of World War II, the Soviet Union had little capital to invest in its industries and the labor force had few machines. Giving a machine to a worker had a huge efficiency payoff, resulting in economic growth. That efficiency payoff and the subsequent high growth stayed high as long as there were workers who needed machines. As a result, during the 1950s, the Soviet economy boasted a period of buoyant growth, sending a chilling message to the free world. But about 1960, the return on machinery investment leveled off as the majority of workers had machines. Further government investment followed, but the returns were zero. The USSR then experienced a steady decline in the rate of growth to investment, from which it didn't recover.

In free market economies, further economic growth came from providing an even higher level of production efficiency. A worker with a drill press, for example, could receive a computerized inventory control system and increase output. A computer could even eliminate the need for a worker. The open market encourages constant independent, entrepreneurial searches for technology to increase and economize production. Such technological advances, when applied to industry, push a country's economic growth. But instead of encouraging the development and use of production-efficient technology, the Soviet Union simply gave the worker with a drill press another drill press. Despite the country's economic growth, the payoff to that growth was virtually nothing. The government continued to invest without seeing a return on the investment. The entire USSR was living off money handed down from Moscow, which eventually proved disastrous.

Caught in the Midst

The breakup of the USSR was a foreign manufacturer's nightmare. One of the few foreign companies manufacturing in the USSR at the time was Tambrands Inc., a UK-based multinational *Fortune* 500 manufacturer of personal care products. Tambrands had been producing tampons near Kiev, Ukraine, for domestic sale. Caught in the midst of the unforeseen breakup of the USSR, Tambrands' actions during the chaotic fundamental political and social changes underline the need for company flexibility.

Tambrands held a 49 percent share in the Kiev operation; the Ukrainian Ministry of Health held 51 percent. After many initial frustrations in the startup phase, the company began running in a fairly predictable manner. Cotton was allocated from a state-run bleachery, delivered to Tambrands' plant and made into tampons. The finished product then went to a government distributor, which distributed the product to state-run pharmacies around the USSR in anticipated quantities. The centralized government in Moscow strictly controlled the market, making sales and marketing virtually unnecessary. Forecasting production was not a major problem.

Soon came the attempted coup in Moscow in August of 1991. The USSR began to quickly disintegrate. Four months later, leaders of the Soviet republics met in Minsk, Byelorussia where they formally divided the Soviet Union into the Commonwealth of Independent States.

The breakup of the USSR—completely unforeseen— immediately impacted on Tambrands' operations. New republics no longer answered to Moscow. They asserted their new autonomy by holding free elections, installing border check-points and printing their own currency. Ministry officials were replaced. Moscow subsidies were cut and economies began to falter. Transportation routes were broken. Tambrands, which had been buying cotton through the centrally planned Soviet system, saw that cotton supplies were endangered.

In order to ensure a high-quality supply of cotton fiber to their Ukrainian operation, the company needed quick solutions. To solve this problem, they bought a bleachery in the former USSR. (A bleachery cleans raw cotton from the fields and then dries it through a specific process so the cotton will maintain its absorbency.) No Tambrands company worldwide had ever run a bleachery before.

About the same time, the rigidly centralized supply system began to fall apart. The CIS was to begin a massive disintegration and restructuring toward a more free market economy. Privatization began on a large scale, and the rouble floated. Buyers, cut off from state subsidies, had no money to buy any more goods. A host of problems including lack of distribution and lack of consumer understanding about the product caused domestic sales to drop by 40 percent in the first few months of 1992.

Tambrands had virtually no sales organization. The supply system in the centralized economy had made a sales team unnecessary. Andy Armenian, vice president of Tambrands' CIS operations, explains:

> As a Western company, we were manufacturing a qual-ity product and making it available in an environment where there were not too many choices for sanitary care. Since we were not tied in to any ministries, people were just lining up at our factory to buy our products. This is one side. On the other side, our sales were limited in Ukraine because of the Ministry of Health regulations. Nearly our entire production was going to the pharma-cies. So between what we were supplying to the pharma-cies, and people showing up to buy, we were selling all our capacity. So there was no need to have a sales organi-zation or marketing. The only thing we had was an educa-tion department that explained how the product was used.

The value of the rouble began dropping daily, sometimes dramatically. Tambrands' customers typically paid slowly and big losses often occurred by the time the money arrived in Tambrands' bank account. Timely collection of money in order to prevent against devaluation became a critical issue.

Tambrands had to act quickly if they wanted to survive in the changing market. It was essential to advertise, educate the consumer about the product, distribute and display the product so it would be visible and recognizable to the consumers. They needed new buyers and new outlets.

What did they have to urgently create? For starters: realistic pricing; a timely payment system; a reliable transportation and distribution system; and departments for sales, advertising and marketing (which were new concepts in the former USSR).

To the company's credit, they not only survived but today can boast an impressive success in the CIS. Tambrands serves as a reminder to foreign companies that Russia's market requires an athletic flexibility, brisk decision making, substantial risk and a long-term attitude.

4
SOVIET BUSINESS CULTURE

Cultural Carryover

Turn over a piece of aluminum cutlery or a plastic object made in Russia and often the price is molded into it. Traditionally, markets were so stable that prices didn't change over decades. Indeed, for the average Russian, the Soviet economic system before Mikhail Gorbachev assumed leadership in the early 1980s appeared to be a grand, predictable, nearly flawless system in which unemployment and depression didn't exist and everyone lived at least comfortably. All able-bodied citizens could readily find jobs. The state guaranteed lifelong employment and the worker was supported from birth until death, provided he didn't try to rebel against the system. But the deeper reality, as the world knew, revealed an iron-fisted ruling body that severely punished initiative, expression, criticism and progress, and kept its workforce in a state of immature dependency.

Today's Russian business culture is essentially the Soviet business culture of yesterday, although fundamental changes to a more Western-style model are under way. But Soviet traditions cannot simply be replaced by Western-style management. The foreign partner must adopt certain parts of the Soviet business culture to the operation to allow for the possibility for success. As one foreign executive says, "In Russia, I am not only a teacher, I'm also a student."

Big Is Beautiful

To get a taste of the Soviet ideological impact on business, witness the tale of Russia's semiconductor industry. For all its brilliant scientists and engineers, Russia's shot at mass manufacturing competitive semiconductor chips for the worldwide market was thwarted by rigid adherence to the Soviet philosophy of the 1940s.

During the late 1970s, when the U.S. knew that semiconductors would be the wave of the future, Soviet President Leonid Brezhnev set up a secret electronics research center in Zelenograd, near Moscow, which became known as the "Silicon Valley of Russia." But instead of encouraging innovative research from Russia's talented engineers, the Soviet government instructed the electronics industry to focus on reverse-engineering of dominant Western products.

The real reason was that tiny microelectronics weren't taken seriously, explains Victor Tsvetov, manager of the microelectronics division, Svetlana Electron Device Manufacturing Co., in St. Petersburg. The Soviet government respected monolithic ideas, projects and technology. Huge iron power generators, for example, were easily accepted as important. "But when they saw a microchip they thought, 'What is it? A tiny little device?' They underestimated the role of microelectronics in shaping the world," Tsvetov says.

As the world electronics industry raced ahead, Russia's industry kept receiving cash infusions to manufacture poor copies of Western microprocessors or memory chips which were already dated by the time they left the factory. No mass production was exportable because of patent infringements. Dated designs of memory chips and microprocessors were virtually useless to local PC assemblers. Any original technology became one of the many underfunded research projects.

In 1988, the Soviet government realized its grave mistake and rushed to erect modern semiconductor plants in the USSR. But a crashing economy and fundamental political changes stopped their complete development. Today, when a country's development is largely determined by technological prowess, Russia must play a serious game of catch-up.

Brawny Factories

The vast Soviet empire underwent mass industrialization during the time of Stalin and Khrushchev, chiefly through the construction of huge factories. Factories were indeed the heart of the former Soviet Union. Large factories produced goods to build the national economy and typically served the national defense by making products for the military. In St. Petersburg, where the bulk of its five million residents were employed in factories, 80 percent of the factories were fulfilling military orders.

To be a laborer in the Soviet Union was comfortably rewarded and initially considered prestigious. Communism was the revolution of the common worker, and the factory was the place where workers engaged in patriotic labor, producing for the state.

A typical factory employed tens of thousands of workers and very often served as a city within a city. Sprawling factory grounds included housing, kindergartens and middle schools, hospitals, shops, a post office, leisure centers, cinemas, sports clubs. They were typically built near water and had their own shipping ports and railway lines. Designed to be self-sufficient complexes, many factories could continue operating even in the event of a wartime attack.

Churning out products for national defense, large factories were also considered strategic military installations. Access was strictly monitored, foreign visitors weren't allowed and photography was forbidden. Some cities, such as Omsk in Central Siberia, which had its whole population churning out secret military-related goods, were essentially "closed" cities, which meant access to the entire city was tightly controlled. Many Russians entered these cities for the first time in the early 1990s, when their top secret status was lifted. Closed cities, once prestigious, now are cities of the unemployed, as defense production fell dramatically after 1991. Many factories have closed, while others teeter on the verge of bankruptcy.

Industry Groups

The Soviet system divided industries into two groups. The *A* group consisted of the military-industrial complex, which received hearty government funding and special privileges such as foreign trade. The *A* group accounted for 70 percent of the government budget. The *B* group was made up of consumer goods manufacturers, considered low priority and low prestige to work for.

An electronics factory, for example, belonged to an *A* group enterprise. The bulk of production of semiconductors, circuit boards and transistors went towards military communication systems and weaponry control systems, while perhaps 20 percent of the products went into radios and televisions for the consumer market. *A* group industries were considered strategic and security was tight.

A beer factory, for example, belonged to the *B* group of industries. It received output figures from the Ministry as well as raw materials and equipment from a government supplies agency. Its finished products were sold through state wholesalers at prices determined by the pricing committee. The beer factory's director and his assistants were mostly involved in negotiating lower output targets and higher supply allocations with government officials. Securing lower production goals would make it easier for employees to get what they wanted: to make enough beer to meet production goals in order to get corresponding bonuses (usually the beer itself).

Central Planning and Quotas

The annual military parade in Red Square was the same every year. As Soviet citizens watched, commanders and troop regiments marched by, tanks and rockets were wheeled along. Predictably, every year the parade ended with a formation of strategic missiles, unchallenged as the most powerfully destructive weapons in the entire Soviet Union.

This year, however, something different happened. After the final huge missiles there suddenly appeared a group of men in raincoats, white shirts and ties, carrying briefcases. Spectators were baffled. "Who are they?" asked one government official. "They are the members of the central planning committee," answered another, "now the strongest force of destruction in the USSR."

At the heart of that old Russian joke was the fact that supply and demand did not determine production output in the Soviet market. Products appeared because the bureaucratic structures controlling production deemed it fit to give certain commodities the go-ahead. Consumer needs were neglected on a macroeconomic scale. If the Central Planning Committee in Moscow decided factories would produce ten million light bulbs, it was not considered necessary to ask consumers what size or strength they would prefer. Because the light bulbs sold out within days, central planning authorities could prove their production specifications were accurate. But in reality, lack of choices, an erratic supply and sometimes shortage of goods was behind the demand. If a consumer hasn't seen a light bulb in the shops for four months and expects another shortage soon, he buys whatever is currently available, regardless of specific needs.

Elementary market research would have easily revealed consumer desires, but was never necessary. Following Soviet philosophy, individual choice did not exist; all citizens' needs were fulfilled by the state in a standardized form. Moreover, if virtually all products were selling out as they hit the stores, there was no incentive to more accurately assess the market—and no consequences for the manufacturer who ignored it. No competition existed. No private companies were allowed to compete with state-run businesses and imports were negligible. With comfortable salaries and an apparently increasing production output, without competition and without a bottom line to protect, Soviet managers simply went with the flow.

Foreign Trade

In past times, no factory could influence its own import-export business. Foreign trade was run at the governmental level and regulated through intergovernmental agreements on trade. Money was allocated for it by the Soviet government. Factories would sell their goods unbelievably cheap overseas in order to impress other countries with the apparently bountiful, generous and prosperous communist system. Huge enterprises conducted foreign trade. There was really no room for middle- and small-size companies.

Subjective decisions shaped Russia's trade policy. For example, if a minister went to Italy and was treated well by an Italian company, he could later decide to conclude a handsome contract with the Italian company. Export worked along similar lines. The various government ministries had lists of the companies they controlled and could distribute export contracts as they pleased. Although ministries would consult with managers in a bilateral process, managers were implementers, not decision makers. Export contracts, like allocations, depended on personal relationships. If a director of one factory was friendly with the ministry official, his factory received the big contract.

Local enterprises had been so dependent on the Ministry of Foreign Trade that when it was eliminated in the 1980s, factories didn't know how to trade. They didn't know how to get their own supplies and find their own markets. Many are still learning today.

Without Distinction

Two professors work at the same university. One is exemplary, devoting unusual attention to the development of his students, assigning demanding homework and making them stretch the limits of their knowledge. The other teacher shows up every day, assigns work and holds students only to what is required. Both teachers will always receive the same pay. This system of equal pay for the same work regardless of individual effort was known as *uravnilovka*. *Uravnilovka* helped destroy the drive to excel.

In the West, each individual tends to strive for independence, distinction, something special that sets the person, employee or company apart from countless others. In Russia, the opposite has been true to an equally extreme degree. The Soviet government emphasized that there is no individual distinction; all are equal. Needless to say, when the population is uniform, it is much easier to rule.

The destruction of distinction began in the early grades and penetrated throughout Soviet society. In kindergarten, children may have been told to draw a picture of a tree. If one child drew a lake and a tree instead, a reprimand was swift and sure. The child was to draw only what the class was drawing. In society, individual inventors were often dismissed as frauds. Soviet artists who won awards could only win once, so the government could give other artists a chance to shine, even if their work was mediocre. Initiative and creativity were strangled.

Uravnilovka was often referred to in a cynical sense to avoid working: Why work when you can get paid for just sitting at a desk? In any case, the system distorted the value of work and was one main reason for shoddy workmanship, falling production output and general economic decline.

Keeping Others Down

Uravnilovka began as a Bolshevik idea intended to crush the greedy capitalist farmer (*kulak*) and redress the enormous gap between rich and poor in Imperial Russia. In the Soviet system, *uravnilovka* encouraged people to take or destroy what others had if it was more than their own.

The Soviet citizen was encouraged to advance communism—not himself. That meant ensuring his neighbor did not get ahead of him. A Russian who was envious of the relative prosperity or success of a friend, neighbor or acquaintance might deliver an anonymous denunciation to the feared KGB. Lives could be ruined with a phone call.

Not only wealth but anything unusual was frowned upon. It was believed that each person of the same social group should look and act similar and have similar opportunities and hopes. Uniqueness fueled civic resentment.

The practice of resenting, discouraging or quashing another's distinction is central to Sovietized Russians. Even something as trivial as a person's mood seems to be affected by *uravnilovka*. The rare Russian who smiles and jokes in public even today often brings disapproving stares from the generally grim majority, who are silently suffering through harsh economic times.

In today's business climate, the practice of *uravnilovka* has a curious effect. A Russian businessman not only desires to continually build his own power base, accumulating money and connections—he also tends to work hard to stop others from gaining power. Competitors or political opponents have traditionally been destroyed by a wide variety of methods, from malicious rumors to brute force.

Feting the Boss

A common Soviet practice which still lingers today was to bring the boss gifts and do him favors. Food and alcohol were typical presents. An employee who feted the boss would get preferential treatment, including time off, a good job assignment and leniency should he fall into trouble.

A woman faced a more complex problem. She was implicitly expected to provide sex if the boss had the inclination. If she complied, her working life would be smooth. If she didn't, thorny difficulties and further harassment were certain until she submitted. A woman who repeatedly refused to consent was often fired.

Much of this tradition remains today. The "Help Wanted" section of any Russian newspaper sometimes frankly specifies "no sex" in an ad placed by a woman looking for work. In foreign companies, foreign managers express astonishment that Russian women employees candidly offer themselves to the boss.

The Man at the Top of the Ladder

Russia has had thousands of years of despotism during which the country was run by a strong male authority figure to whom obedience was essential for survival. Even before the Soviet era, there was scant history of political freedom or majority rule in Russian politics. No tradition of self-reliance and independent thinking exists.

Family life has always been strictly patriarchal and similar attitudes were reflected in society at large. Russia could be seen as a large family with a ruling czar, a stern father figure who led the country, correcting or punishing those who strayed from his dictates. This layer of vertical decision making was inherited by the Bolsheviks, who quickly installed a dictatorship.

So it's no surprise that Soviet companies contained a strict vertical structure, with the concentration of decision making in one or a very few hands. Whether it was a tractor factory or the huge travel enterprise Intourist, a man typically sat at the top of the hierarchical ladder. Russia's management structures, compared to international standards, haven't changed since they were installed after the Revolution of 1917.

In the Russian version, power is concentrated in very few hands, usually with only one person, who figuratively sits at the top of the ladder. The vertical structure impairs company communication between various junior levels in the company because information needs to pass up the steps and then down again, rather than directly across. Remove a key employee, perhaps because of illness or a holiday, and the operations could rapidly grind to a halt. The ladder structure is evident even today in the simple example of the company stamp. Every contract, payment or letter concluded by a Russian company must bear the company stamp. In most companies only one such stamp exists. It, and often the signature of the director, must be on even the most trivial of documents—for instance a form authorizing a secretary to go and pick up a stationery order. A common excuse for the nonpayment of bills in Russia is the absence of the company director.

The Soviet company director was a senior Communist Party member, often handpicked by friends in the government ministry which supervised the particular industry, following Russia's deeply ingrained tradition of patronage. The director worked closely with the government to meet Moscow-dictated production quotas and follow government directives related to his business. His status and power were typically measured by how many employees were under his direction. He didn't have to please legions of consumers or shareholders, look nervously over his shoulder at the competition, nor keep up on current market trends and product innovations.

Freed from the time-consuming pursuit of a handsome bottom line, the director had plenty of executive energy left over to engage in power plays, perhaps laying the groundwork for his next promotion—or sabotaging the advancement of a rival. He usually set the tone for the level of intrigue in his company. The excessive number of middle managers maneuvered vigorously to try and gain his favor. Time-consuming discussions, reports and recommendations between director and manager often had no practical value; they were simply sheer political gamesmanship.

Today the foreign businessman should be aware that the Russian workplace remains highly politicized, with rampant gossip, favoritism and intrigue commonplace.

Decisions, Decisions

During the totalitarian Soviet era, the ingredient of fear was added to the national psyche. Generations were brought up knowing the danger involved in acting or even thinking independently. Stalin's paranoia, the growth and widespread influence of the terrifying KGB and frequent Cold War conspiracies helped create a society based on secrecy and suspicion. George Orwell's totalitarian nightmare novel *1984* was based largely on the Soviet Union. In Soviet Russia, lives were ruined and people were imprisoned or shot for mild transgressions of the established order—or even for not being zealous enough conformists. Naturally, the workplace was affected.

Needless to say, decision making could be a very dangerous practice. Fear of the consequences left many people loathe to make any decision if it could be passed upwards instead, reinforcing the vertical structure. Further, in a highly centralized society, most decisions are made for the populace by those in the seats of power. Government directives could not be analyzed and opposed. Critical thinking was virtually forbidden. Options were few, if any. All these factors came together and helped create an innate aversion to decision making.

Today, foreign businessmen describe the unwillingness to make decisions as the Russian manager's greatest obstacle. "We're still trying to sort out the good managers from the bad," says a foreign executive of a U.S. company that bought a Russian factory.

> To sort them out, you put the manager into a position where he has to make a decision. That's one thing about the old central planning, it took away the thinking, the decision making. Nobody had to make a decision, everything was made for them. Now they're in a position where

they have to make decisions, right or wrong, and they're just scared. You have to force them to make a decision. At first it's difficult. You cannot trust them to make the correct decision, so you're doubling up on your workload. If they make a mistake, you have to correct the mistake, then you have to put them into another position where they have to make another decision, which may mean another mistake. Sometimes it works.

Moreover, Russians, accustomed to one choice only, are baffled and nervous in the face of many options. When *perestroika* allowed Russians to travel outside the country for the first time, they often came back and reported they were shocked by all the options and subsequent decisions necessary in Western life. Walking into an ice cream shop with thirty-one flavors creates a kind of mental paralysis in those not used to a multitude of choices.

On the company level, it is sometimes necessary to spell out to a Russian employee specifically what should be done. A Western businessperson running a joint venture in St. Petersburg tells how he asked an employee to buy paper for a laser printer. It didn't matter what kind, the manager said, as long as the paper went in one end and came out the other. But many different types of paper were available, the employee couldn't decide and the paper wasn't purchased—until the exact type was specified.

Decision making includes the chance of making mistakes—but mistakes are closely associated with danger in Russia.

The Russian Worker

Russian workers run the gamut from excellent to poor, just like any other workforce in the world. But one difference is that Russian people have worked for decades in a system which gave little reward for hard work and didn't punish sloth. Well-chosen, well-led, and correctly motivated Russian employees are often excellent, but, for unprepared outsiders, they will seem to have maddening characteristics unique to their culture.

German sociologist Jurgen Feldhof conducted studies of several German-Russian manufacturing ventures and discovered some key differences between the two sides. He points out that the Russian worker wants a place of emotional atmosphere where people understand him, where he can talk about his wife, fishing, rising prices and where he will be understood. Often he wants a manager or foreman to accept him in a familiar way. He wants work to feel like home and he needs time on the job to chat with others despite work obligations. But the Russian worker doesn't understand that in the West the home and work atmosphere seldom have fundamental similarities.

Russian workers are typically unaware and unconcerned about the bigger economic picture, a possible cause of friction with management. For example, the foreign boss of a growing company told a Russian sales representative that profit would first go toward sorely needed equipment purchases, then later to salary hikes. "I know what you're doing," she protested. "I've read Marx. You're an exploiter." While management judged that lack of expansion would blunt its competitive edge, the Russian employee couldn't see the larger picture outside the worker's sphere. Along the same lines, more Russian employees are beginning to expect high wages and some sort of workplace democracy at foreign firms.

In the Soviet tradition, when Russian workers met yearly production goals, bonus money was split among them. Because Russians are used to group bonuses for collective achievement, wage differentials or individually negotiated contracts often create friction. The employee earning more money than his colleagues will likely breed envy, dislike and factionalism among staff.

But contrary to collective reward, collective responsibility hasn't been ingrained. The Russian worker does not feel he's responsible for anything other than his own familiar tasks. Foreign businesspeople say one frustrating characteristic of Russian employees is the resulting compartmentalization approach to work. One worker may sit idle while another struggles, inundated by work. The first will explain that he has finished his work, and that the work that remains is the specialty of the other—even though it's obvious that anyone could do it, specialist or not. The notorious shop clerks in old state-run department stores were known for standing idly while customers jammed the shop because their job didn't involve waiting on customers. The problem is complicated by the enforced inefficiency of Soviet times. When company staff was padded to employ all citizens, it became important to find enough work for all. That meant making sure that each worker did his own specific share of work—and only his own.

Demarcation is a strong feature of the Russian workplace. The concept of the "all-around" employee is rare. A worker assigned to work at a certain job may be loathe to move temporarily outside his normal orbit to another point, even if the move will improve overall efficiency.

Thousands of years of despotism has taught Russians to respond to force in the form of a strongman. Westerners may respect a commandeering figure, but they also expect him to listen and respond thoughtfully to others and demand that his power be held in check by other institutions or organizations. In Russia, however, a tolerant leader is often seen as weak. In the workplace, the easygoing, liberal boss may be tested by employees who see his patience as a weakness. A foreign manager tells the story of a Russian employee who suddenly announced her vacation at a crucial time in the company's production schedule. The placid manager had tried extensive one-on-one talks concerning the importance of the employee's work to the company, with no result. When he lashed out with a scathing verbal rebuke, overnight the employee's attitude underwent a marked change for the better.

While it's not fair to say all workers respond to anger, Russian employees do often want to recognize strength in their authority figure. The Russian worker generally feels familiar with a blustery, gruff but fair boss who tells employees what to do rather than coaxes or suggests. The boss should be capable of displaying his power in order to be respected. "The Russian workers like being shouted at once in a while," says a British manager of a factory in St. Petersburg. "I don't like doing that. But they actually come to me and tell me to shout at them!"

In professional roles, Russian employees tend to use serious rhetoric and enthusiasm as a mask for lack of training and experience. Historical roots for this practice extend back to the Communist Party administration. In the early Soviet state, revolutionary fervor was considered vastly more important than administrative experience. As the Soviet system evolved, senior administrators moved with the party, rather than with a company or industry. A person might run a village, then a tourist resort, and later a huge industrial complex. It was more important to display fervent political beliefs and appear a staunch conformist in the eyes of high party functionaries, than to have racked up administrative successes and acquired a depth of experience.

Don't Rock the Boat

In Soviet times, workers who did something grossly illegal could be fired. But workers who simply worked badly or were constantly late might only lose holiday bonuses or other benefits. They were virtually impossible to fire. Incentive schemes were not used. There was little reason to work harder than others, nor was there any particular reason to produce quality work.

Managers and staff devoted energy to pleasing those in the government, creating a workplace atmosphere referred to as *spakoistvi* (serenity). *Spakoistvi* did not necessarily depend on meeting quotas or doing a job well. It depended largely on employee behavior. A radio station manager, for example, would not care what percentage of the listening audience the station held or whether the programs were lively or interesting. The overriding concern was that no employee said anything politically dubious or played any so-called decadent Western music. Given that scenario, the quality of broadcasts was less important than employing staff who could be relied upon to keep the company serene.

In sectors less sensitive than the media, *spakoistvi* might be judged in other ways. Shop managers, for example, had an undersupplied (and so, captive) market, ensuring nearly effortless sales. Moreover, companies had an overabundance of employees, resulting from the Soviet law requiring every citizen of able mind and body to hold a job or face legal prosecution. The shop's *spakoistvi* came from doing only what was required. It had little interest in acquiring quality products, arranging eye-catching displays or providing enthusiastic service. The prevailing company attitude held that times were good—so why risk doing anything different?

The unwillingness to change is a formidable obstacle today. Arvind Sachdev, Sales Manager of Tambrands' CIS Operations, manufacturer of Tampons, recalls how he went to stores around Russia and tried to increase sales. "Say we were selling ten cases of Tampax a month in a store. We told our buyers that they could sell fifteen per month if they put the product on the shelf, on display. They would say 'Oh no, we have been selling it very well. Why should we put it on the shelf? Why should you worry about it?' "

Service Without a Smile

The quest for serenity, rather than profit, helped shape the Soviet business culture. In heavy industry, searching for new customers was unnecessary, since the government was buying the output. In the retail and service industry, demand outpaced supply and employees received no commissions or bonuses for selling. All the salesclerk was encouraged to do was exert a minimum level of effort. Firing employees for being rude to customers, for example, was virtually impossible because the government wanted to maintain full employment levels. The only incentive was to go with the immense, inefficient system. "Communism goes like this," says an old Russian joke. "They pretend to pay us and we pretend to work."

The resulting business culture, in which consumers often had to fight to gain services or products, is central to the understanding of the development of Russian business today. The appalling treatment that tourists to Soviet Russia used to laugh about was a day-to-day experience for millions of Russian consumers. Even today, poor service lingers: Phones are answered rudely; receptionists, shop assistants, waiters and others are unhelpful; product choice is kept limited; contracts are fulfilled late and products of poor quality are not backed by guarantees.

Customer service is alien to the Soviet business culture. Yet in the post-*perestroika* business era there is a growing realization of the value of service. The beginning of a shift from a docile to a more demanding client is being accompanied by a shift in employee perceptions of clients. Some employees are reacting to management attempts to instill a pride in their companies, but more are reacting to the specter of unemployment. Russia's era of guaranteed employment is over. Overstaffed businesses are beginning to be downsized. Bad workers are starting to be replaced by good ones. And with the safety net of the state now in tatters, the prospect of losing a job is a serious incentive. Nonetheless few Russian businesses have yet made a link between service and success. The phrase *consumers' rights* tends to bring looks of puzzlement when translated into Russian.

5

CONTEMPORARY RUSSIA

Life Somewhere Between East and West

Clustered Living

Russia is roughly one-tenth of the world, with wide-open spaces stretching for thousands of miles, covering eleven time zones. Yet the bulk of the 150 million people lives in generic concrete apartment buildings clustered inside cities, from the border of Scandinavia to the Far East. The blocks of flats, resulting from a construction surge during the buildup of the Soviet Union, vary little and reflect the Soviet characteristics of standardization, communality and sweeping vision. Stand-alone houses are rare in cities.

Soviet citizens were awarded an apartment according to family size, together with a small plot of land outside the city on which they could construct a *dacha* (country cottage) or simply grow vegetables. Weekends, especially in the summer, the family often travels to the *dacha* to tend to their garden or just relax with friends.

Today, the state is slowly transferring ownership of most apartments to Russians through privatization. But living space has become a headache. Today, when children grow up and marry, they must rent or buy flats, which can be too costly for the young Russian family. Before, they could apply to the government for a free apartment. As a result, most young couples today end up living with their parents under cramped conditions. In large cities, apartment rental markets have blossomed. Older people are moving in with relatives and renting their flats to young couples as a source of vital income.

To Russians, the flat is more than a physical living space; it's regarded as a sanctuary from the hard life on the street. A Russian will often shift into a sullen street mode when leaving the flat, or be uplifted upon arrival home. An invitation to a Russian's flat is a great honor. Not just anybody is invited inside.

The first-time visitor may be surprised that the family has spent their whole life in such a modest place. Shoes will be lined up at the doorway, as those who enter are expected to wear house slippers, which the host provides. The flat's furniture and interior decor will likely be outmoded. The telephone, for example, could be a rotary dial phone designed in the 1970s. There probably won't be simple home efficiency machines such as a washer or microwave oven. The couch will double as a bed. Shelves and shelves of books—novels and encyclopedias—often line the walls. Russians are readers. The typical Russian family are lovers of books and the children have spent more time reading books than watching television.

Population Redistribution

Throughout periods of Russia's history millions of citizens were uprooted and forced to move around the country. Many families, originally from villages or the country's far reaches, ended up in big cities.

Shipping prisoners from the big cities to work camps in unpopulated stretches of Siberia was a favorite practice of Russian czars. After serving time, many prisoners remained in the area, had families and built small cities. The city of Omsk in Central Siberia, for example, was a bare patch of tundra along a river until prisoners—many simply dissidents or suspected conspirators—were sent there to live and work in a prison colony. Dostoyevsky served time there in the nineteenth century, sentenced by the czar for his role in distributing underground publications which were deemed to be treasonous to Russia.

Later, Stalin's infamous deportations, officially sanctioned starvation, executions and paranoid search for enemies of the state forced tens of millions of Soviet citizens from their homes. Intellectuals, artists, and wealthy families either immigrated, or were executed or shipped to far reaches of Russia. Peasants from the village were sent or encouraged to come to the big cities.

In accordance with the idea of a workers' revolution, many uneducated people were installed in key positions of education, business and government. Lacking the experience and education, they often created havoc in the institutions they served. Mute resentment among the populace festered. To this day, Russians in St. Petersburg, for example, always want to know if a new acquaintance had grandparents who were born in St. Petersburg or elsewhere. Those without longstanding roots in the city are often judged to be descendants of transplanted peasant stock.

Different Status

Soviet citizens were rigidly defined by the social category they were in. Each category had a certain standard of living and level of prestige. *Nomenklatura* was the highest level of social group. Politicians, top bureaucrats and high Communist Party members were typical *nomenklatura*. These people were a privileged, small percent of the population. Their families were wealthier than the average Soviet family and they held influential jobs. Many were given special privileges such as high-level medical care, foreign travel and study, prestigious living accommodations and the purchase of foreign goods. Education was not a determining factor for *nomenklatura*. Like Imperial Russia's ruling elite, they often received their posts through connections.

Today, many *nomenklatura* have become wealthy new businesspeople by virtue of their influence and connections. Power and status has not left their hands. *Nomenklatura* includes top people in the government, military and industry.

The next level of privilege went to a small group of specialists who played a direct role in maintaining or glorifying the Soviet system. These included KGB officials, special engineers and technicians engaged in the space program and weapons development, a small percent of artists and intellectuals used for propaganda purposes and sportsmen who would travel and compete in the name of the USSR.

Next came the bulk of the Soviet population: the proletariat, typically a factory worker or person involved in physical labor that didn't require much expertise. Ample salaries ensured that the proletariat lived reasonably well. Since most goods and services were free or heavily subsidized, the bulk of the worker's paycheck was disposable income. Such workers made up the masses and they had few privileges.

Underneath the proletariat were the *intelligentsiya* and average engineers and technicians. *Intelligentsiya* included actors, writers, artists, professors, musicians and the like. Since this group was concerned with ideas, expression and independent thinking, they had to be strictly monitored. Privileges were rare, surveillance was typical and pay was only enough to live on.

Average engineers and technicians at the same level as the intelligensia were instrumental in keeping the military-industrial complex churning. They worked with their minds more than their hands and, keeping with Bolshevik traditions, received less pay than those engaged in physical labor.

Toward the lower end of the economic scale were country farmers or peasants. Peasant families lived in the villages and farmed to supply the state-run collectives with crops. According to one theory, the party elite bore a grudge against peasants and kept their pay low because many didn't support the proletariat revolution. Some peasants had been rich land owners, and many had taken part in the counterrevolution. Peasants' families typically remained uneducated for generations.

At the lowest point were the destitute—alcoholics, the mentally and physically handicapped, political dissidents and the chronically unemployed.

Ranking the standard of living in the USSR:

Top 20 percent
   Nomenklatura: politicians, top bureaucrats
   High-ranking military
   Specialists vital to the system

Remaining 80 percent
Proletariat
Intelligentsiya, engineers and technicians
Peasants
Destitute

Ranking the standard of living in today's Russia:

Top 20 percent

New businessmen: bankers, speculators, criminals
Nomenklatura: politicians, top military figures, high bureaucrats, industry chieftains
Special law enforcement troops: anticriminal squads, border
police, customs and tax inspectors

Remaining 80 percent
Small business owners
Intelligentsiya
Proletariat
Retired people
Destitute

Education

Russia's system of free education and literacy rate of 99 percent
indicates a relatively well-educated population. Compulsory
education ends at age sixteen but nearly all people complete
some form of study beyond that age. In fact, the percentage
of dropouts is significantly lower than in the U.S. The quality
of Russian teaching in science and math, especially theoretical
instruction, tends to be higher than in Western countries.
Social sciences, however, are just beginning to be taught.

Competing for a place in university is highly intense. Educa-
tors say that in the past excellent entrance exam scores and a
little *svyazi* (connections) would often secure a place for an aspi-
rant. Today the same people say what matters most is *svyazi*
plus generosity in the form of cash, especially when applying
to prestigious departments such as foreign languages or law.

Those that don't enter university have ample second
choices. Russia is full of institutes and polytechnics. For learn-

ing practical skills, there is the *technikum* (to become a mechanic, for example), the *professionalnaya uchilsya* (tailor, carpenter, etc.) and many new short, intensive courses specializing in skills related to secretarial work, the insurance industry, management or public relations.

Military

Once the proud defenders of a world superpower, counterbalancing the formidable armed forces of the West, Soviet soldiers enjoyed the admiration and warm support of the citizenry. Today, becoming a Russian soldier is a dreaded inevitability for most young men, and worth avoiding at all costs. Pay is abominably low, accommodations and equipment are deteriorating and corruption is rife. Even worse, recruits are subjected to brutal hazing rituals (*diedovshchyna*), which have scandalized the military and caused the deaths of numerous young men. Concerned mothers have even organized groups to lobby for reform and humane treatment of recruits.

In principle, every Russian male of able body and mind must serve at least two years in the military. Exemptions are made for students in higher education during the period of study; afterward the government can call them up for national service, if needed. But the young Russian man typically checks every avenue of escape possible to avoid being drafted.

Since the debacle in Afghanistan—often labeled "Russia's Vietnam"—from which Russia withdrew after ten years of fighting, the entire defense apparatus has deteriorated. Since the late 1980s, deep defense cuts were made. As hordes of Russian troops were brought back from Eastern Europe and the Baltic States, the beleaguered Russian government couldn't provide accommodations or jobs. Many soldiers deserted, were recruited by organized crime, or sold military weapons and equipment on the black market. Meanwhile, Western armies made significant breakthroughs into the era of highly accurate "smart" weaponry.

The state of the military was evident in the bloody fighting in the small breakaway republic of Chechenya. A relatively small group of Chechenyan fighters managed to hold off elite

Russian army units for weeks in the battle to capture the capital city of Grozny. Moreover, reports of attempted mutiny and high-level infighting led to the bombing of the army's own troops.

Military life is no longer prestigious, but top officials such as the defense minister and high generals still wield impressive power and influence in the government.

Leisure

Russians spend a considerable amount of their leisure time at the homes of friends and relatives. Sharing food, drink, conversation and perhaps dancing and singing with friends in the home seems to be the most popular pastime, for they seldom like to be alone.

A lack of quality restaurants and bars kept Russians home in the past; today economic constraints work to the same effect. Moreover, Russians tend to associate in specific social circles. They feel that meeting at restaurants, surrounded by strangers, prevents real relaxation. As a result, the bar or nightclub culture that exists in many foreign countries is absent from Russia.

Theater, orchestral concerts and the ballet have been immensely popular in the big cities. Cinemas have fallen from popularity as the strong initial impact of new television programming and videoplayers has yet to wear off. But the majority of Russians don't watch television, and prefer passing their spare time with friends rather than being spectators.

Few Russians have cars and those who do seldom use them for leisure pursuits. A usual sight is families or friends taking commuter trains to someone's *dacha* in the countryside. Russians are a people traditionally close to nature. Swimming, camping, fishing or walking in the woods tend to be popular pastimes.

Even in the winter, the *dacha* is a place for ice skating, ice fishing or skiing. Just as European children were usually taught soccer and American children basketball, Russian children were taught how to ski. The vast majority of Russians learned how to both downhill and cross-country ski.

Religion

The belief in a higher power and the promise of a glorious future has always been a notable unifying characteristic of Russians. During aristocratic rule, the church and state were inextricably linked. After the Revolution, the communist government replaced the supreme being. Religion was crushed under the Soviet fist until the 1980s, when Mikhail Gorbachev began reestablishing ties to the Orthodox church, returning confiscated property and allowing for freedom of worship.

Today Russian Orthodoxy is the country's main religion, followed by Islam, Catholicism, Protestantism and Judaism. Religion has enjoyed a modest resurgence, but most Russians don't seem to adhere strictly to any religion, and many say they do not believe in any higher power. The prevalence of superstitions and the rising popularity of astrology indicates a large spiritual vacuum.

Infrastructure

Until 1991, it was faster to take a five-hour train ride from St. Petersburg to Finland to make an international phone call than be put on the three-day waiting list by the St. Petersburg operator.

In an ironic twist, today domestic calls are often more difficult to make than those abroad. It is now possible to call the United States, Europe and Australia in seconds, but still spend an hour trying to dial a neighboring Russian town. Phone traffic has increased between Russia's two largest cities, but the domestic phone system has remained the same and can't handle the overload. Meanwhile, foreign telecom companies have been busy upgrading international lines.

The easiest and most frequent target of complaints is Russia's ramshackle infrastructure. Much of Russia's physical infrastructure hasn't been updated for decades. The visitor immediately and vividly experiences the slow, rickety bus crammed with people, the potholed roads, and broken pay phones. Those straying from Moscow find businesses with manual typewriters rather than computers; carbon paper rather than a photocopier; hospitals with glass syringes rather than plastic throwaways and ambulances fitted with only the most rudimentary of equipment. Interior decor in many shops

and offices is outdated and many buildings have been left to decay. In fact, visitors have remarked that Russia hasn't changed its wardrobe since 1970.

Russia's surface appearance and day-to-day discomforts tend to catch the critical eye of Westerners, especially Americans who are used to convenient living. Yet things are changing. As foreign companies flood into the country and form joint ventures, the infrastructure is slowly upgrading in the larger cities. In Moscow and St. Petersburg, foreign telecom companies have set up joint ventures with Russian ones and are in the process of modernizing the network.

Transport networks exist but are in urgent need of repair and expansion. Buses and trams are old and demand great patience from people who wait for them. The highway system is largely undeveloped, and the railroad network is extensive but needs repair and upgrading. Aeroflot, the former state-owned airline, which once boasted the largest number of flying routes in the world, serving the vast Soviet Union, suffers from frequent fuel shortages, poor maintenance procedures and lack of money and equipment. The company has been decentralized and some small-scale domestic competitors have popped up.

The social infrastructure faces a far more difficult time. Law enforcement, education, health care, social services, museums and the arts are some of the services in a state of crisis resulting from a radical drop in government subsidies. Young people today are reluctant to enter these vital fields as a university professor, doctor and police sergeant may make the equivalent of $200 per month while someone selling flowers on the street could make the same in a few days.

Emerging from the Image Coma

Positron in St. Petersburg, one of the largest electronics factories in Russia, recently showed a fresh new Positron television set to potential Western buyers at an exposition. One European company was interested in importing them for sale to fashion-conscious consumers because of the marketable "retrostyle." The television hadn't had a design change since the mid-1950s.

Soviet-made products had little emphasis on design. The product's size, strength and functionality—an interesting manifestation of Soviet philosophy, was most important. Moreover, design innovation was unnecessary. Soviet Russia had no consumer market, because the government set production quotas and dictated product development. One common remark from first-time visitors concerns the blandness of architecture, fashion and product design throughout Russia.

Now that a torrent of imported products sparkles in shops and on television, a growing portion of Russians desperately want to own and display them, even though their meager wages allow only limited purchases. Some say the young Russians are experiencing an explosive reaction to the drab Soviet times.

Image is of growing importance, mainly with the younger generation. Russian office staff puzzle over foreigners who sometimes dress casually in jeans and a T-shirt. To young Russians, work is a place to flaunt new suits and dresses. The young Russian man covets a CD player, color television and imported luxury car. The young woman may spend her entire monthly salary on a costly imported sweater.

Ostentation is partially a habit from Soviet times. Sociologist Elena Scherschneva at the University of St. Petersburg believes that, "The Soviet man lived something like a child. He didn't pay for anything—apartment, school, even the telephone was free. He had money to spend, and he would buy anything— food, clothes, a car, a *dacha*. There was no reason to put it in a bank. The only time you needed money was for a wedding or funeral. Now if a Russian man has money, he wants to spend it fast." Often people in the West, she adds, try to downplay their wealth by avoiding flashy badges of success. But Russians with money prefer to show the world they have it.

Other social commentators insist that flashy displays of wealth are rooted in Russian culture. During centuries of monarchy, when a small percentage reveled in the finest fashions and food and a decadent lifestyle, the bulk of the population could only look, dream and nurture their desires.

Names

During Soviet times *Tovarisch* (Comrade) was the label of address. That word has fallen from grace but no formal title of address appeared to replace it. Some use of the pre-Revolutionary *Gospadin* (Gentleman) and *Gospazha* (Madam) is beginning, although this usage is still rare. Mr., Mrs., and Miss, spoken in English, also can be heard occasionally.

To show respect to another in formal address, Russians today commonly speak only the first name plus the patronymic name. In Russia, a girl adopts her father's first name and converts the ending, usually to *-ovna*. So Elena, with a father named Alexander, becomes Elena Alexandrovna. Men adopt their fathers' first names as well, but they commonly use the ending *-vich*. Boris, with a father named Victor, becomes Boris Victorvich.

Use of the patronymic often shows the level of acquaintance between two people. When talking to someone for the first time, or when meeting an acquaintance, superior, or older person, always use the first name together with the patronymic, such as Boris Victorvich. It shows respect. As you become better acquainted with the person, only the first name will be used. In the workplace, communication of lower level to higher level should always use the first name and patronymic.

Russians love nicknames and the complex and voluble Russian language is well-suited for such invention. Just about everyone and everything has at least one nickname, usually made by shortening the word or adding an ending. For men, Dmitri becomes Dima, Alexander becomes Sasha. For women's names, the diminutive has many variations. Elena becomes Lenotchka, Lenoosik, Lenka, Lenchik; Mariana becomes Masha, Mashinka, Mashka, Maschik. Each nickname implies a different degree of softness and can suggest the current relationship between the two people. Even things have nicknames: A bone is *kost*, a little bone is *kostichka*; a *magazin* is a store, a *magazinchik* is a little store; and an *arbuz* is a watermelon but an *arbuzik* is a "little chubby watermelon."

Finally, the foreign visitor should know that Russians seem to have an uncanny ability to remember people's names, even if only heard once. So the foreigner who forgets the name of his Russian friend could be delivering a wallop of an insult.

Food

Food is central to Russian culture. Many families grow their own vegetables on their plot of land and live off the food they have grown. Potatoes, cabbage and carrots are most typical. Home canning of fruits such as peaches and berries is popular. Rarely do families visit restaurants or buy pre-cooked food. Russians believe food is life. Indeed, some tend to discuss the home cultivation of vegetables affectionately, as if they were speaking about raising children. Usually the woman rules food preparation. She is indeed an expert. With one glance at a food market stall she can name an exotic fruit or discern the freshness of a vegetable. It goes without saying that the Russian woman is an accomplished cook. Dinner at midday is normally a family ritual with several homemade courses, beginning with snacks and followed by soup, salad, a main course and dessert. Food is sliced and displayed decoratively.

Within the family, there is little waste. Nearly everything is reused rather than discarded: stale bread is for a friend or relative who owns chickens on the *dacha;* bad milk is boiled and used for cooking; and old jars store food. If newspapers aren't needed for wrapping garbage, they can be used in the fireplace at the *dacha.* Plastic bottles become containers for homemade drinks, and plastic bags are sometimes washed and reused.

Russian Families

The average Russian family has one child. Large families common to the nobility during pre-Revolutionary times have nearly disappeared. Wars, famine and the poor economy have made young parents settle on one child.

Roles within the family are strictly defined: The mother raises the children and runs the household, and she is often the greatest influence on the children. Russian women say their job also includes raising the husband, whom they say is a child inside. For his part, the husband brings home the money and makes key decisions.

Russian families tend to be much closer emotionally than those in the U.S. and some European countries. Rebelliousness and flagrant disrespect is minimal by comparison. Foreign guests will be surprised that Russian children, even teenagers, enjoy singing and dancing with their parents. A seemingly inherent trust between parents and child is striking. Generally, parents tend not to interrogate their children or pry deeply into their private lives; for their part, Russian children will rarely tell lies to their parents.

Children are not encouraged to do things for themselves at an early age. Instead, they tend to be doted on by the parents, especially the mother. An ordinary and socially acceptable situation is grown, unmarried children supported by the parents and living in the same apartment.

Russian parents always see their children as kids, even if those children are forty years old. They still want to see them every day. When children grow up and get married, they seldom leave the city and often remain comfortably close to their parents in every sense.

Man to Woman

Soviet philosophy taught that both sexes were equal companions in an historical struggle toward a classless society. The ideology is reflected in Socialist art, which portrays men and women as serious and muscular, striving forward, looking skyward, side by side.

Some of this ideology transferred to the workplace. Many Russian women entered various engineering fields, but politics, law and law enforcement and high-level management has always been the domain of Russian men. Moreover, distribution of jobs not requiring education followed patriarchal tradition. Women received service-oriented jobs in positions such as shop clerks, light cleaning and cooking, while men received jobs involving machinery and physical labor such as plumbing, driving, mechanical maintenance or warehouse work. Even today, with foreign joint ventures bringing in new sales ideas, the job separation system prevails. Women employees still fill most Russian food shops and the bulk of vehicles on the roads are driven by men.

In reality, the average Russian man's attitude is patriarchal. He holds the innate belief that a woman's main functions are caring for the children, cooking, cleaning and sex. He is expected to make family decisions; consensus is rare. The Russian man does not like his authority challenged. The strictly defined spheres of husband and wife seldom overlap.

A Russian man can also display sweeping passion. Romance often dominates over rationality, and he'll break rules standing in the way of his desires. If he's at a party with good friends, problems are cast aside. He'll bestow flowers and attention on female guests, and may sing from the heart, gush with sentimental praise, drink to excess or dance without inhibition. He believes his excesses are part of being a Russian man and should be forgiven even if they overstep the limits of propriety.

On one hand the Russian woman is tough, practical and sensible. She works physically hard, buying food, cooking, washing the family's clothes by hand, keeping the house clean, which establishes order. On the other hand, she is genuinely moved by conventional displays of beauty such as flowers, colorful packages (even if it's some food product wrapping), pastries and chocolate. Sentimental music and colorful fashions woo her, but unlike the Russian man, her excesses are restrained by her duty to the family. As the voice of reason, she often keeps the family together.

Divorced Together

In Russia, divorced couples commonly live in the same apartment because they cannot find or afford another living place. Waiting lists for new apartments are years long and often there is simply nowhere else to go. Many live together for years, often in the same room. The enormous emotional toll involved hardly needs explanation.

In recent years the living situation has become even more complicated because of the option to privatize apartments. The paperwork may be daunting, but the state will give the apartment away to those who are registered to live at a specific address. Once the place is privatized, a divorced couple may each legally own half of the flat! Cooperation must continue until they agree to sell it outright and split the cash, or try to exchange it for two rooms, each in separate buildings. Apartments and rooms in communal apartments can be swapped with others in similar situations and the classified ads section of local papers describes many living spaces offered for exchange.

While some people are forced to live together, others choose to do so for mutual advantage. A stranger in town wishing to stay needs a precious document called a *propiska*, or permission to reside in a specific city. The *propiska* system was used to monitor the Soviet population and control mobility.

Every Russian has a legal address registered with their local police department. That legal address is noted in a Russian's internal passport, an important document frequently required when dealing with any bureaucracy or agency. Without a *propiska* for the desired city, a Russian will be denied the right to reside there and may be forced to return to his home city.

However, Russians have developed ways to get around this problem. One common method is for a Russian from another city to marry a local strictly to receive a *propiska*; document in hand, the couple divorce. Money is usually paid to the temporary spouse for the service.

The Riddle of Russian Character

The average Russian will beam with a satisfied smile when someone asks for a description of the Russian character. Indefinable, they will say. Russians are staunchly proud of what much of the world believes to be their inner inscrutability. The paraphrase of Winston Churchill's famous description of

Russia as a "mystery wrapped in an enigma," seems to have become conventional wisdom in the West.

It's easy to see why. Holy Russia, before communism, was steeped in superstition and mystery rooted in old pagan traditions. Then came centuries of monarchic rule, linked to the Orthodox church, during which a tiny percent of the population received an education. The ensuing decades of the iron-fisted, secretive Soviet state had the effect of imposing an ideological template over existing Russian character. Clearly, the Soviet system was so influential that a "Soviet" is difficult to distinguish from a "Russian" and many persons will insist that they are the same. Complicating the issue was the restriction on self-exploration which, according to Soviet ideology, was practiced only by decadent individuals bereft of a higher purpose; communism explained all human motivations. Sociology, psychology and other liberal arts, free from government influence, only began in the 1990s.

The mystery will prevail, but some prominent characteristics begin to give the outsider an impression of the Russian character:

Extremism.   Understanding Russians means being aware of the Russian tendency toward extremes rather than incremental growth. Russians carry reserves of patience foreigners would likely consider inexhaustible. But when a Russian reaches a limit, an explosion of change results. There is typically no step-by-step process toward a goal. As the Russian saying goes, "Not until the thunder sounds, does a man make the sign of the cross."

For example, in less than a decade the vast country jumped from imperious aristocracy, where a tiny percentage enjoyed privilege while the majority were in poverty; to the brutal dictatorship of Stalin, who dished out power and privilege to the uneducated masses and executed those considered elite. Today, some commentators warn that the country may follow the traditional pattern and spring back to a pre-Revolutionary strong-armed rule by the wealthy few.

On an individual level, thrusting between extremes is perhaps apparent in the notorious "Russian mood," when a person swings from pleasant to sullen for a seemingly slight reason. In reality, emotions have been building up for a long while.

Emotional approach. Russians generally regard feelings to be more important than facts. A Russian may judge a person more by a gut feeling than by the person's background or potential. Statistics and numbers take a back seat to sentiment.

Moreover, the Russian believes that strong feelings should be expressed, regardless of propriety. If a Russian dislikes someone, he will often say so directly. They are known to burst with honest declarations of their feelings. Social class, breeding and character do not necessarily play a key role in keeping a man's temper under control. If an argument is unavoidable, Russians do not believe it should be conducted in calm, rational tones. An angry boss may shout at employees in front of visitors. The Russian person believes restricting emotions that demand immediate expression is unnatural and dishonest.

Grandeur. The Russian prefers strong, sweeping generalizations to tiny details. Projects and ideas will be envisioned on a huge scale. Such visionary projects have helped to build Russia, from Peter the Great's incredible plan to build a European capital in St. Petersburg to the abundant massive factories with their huge production output that functioned as the heart of the former Soviet Union. But these grand visions tend to disregard the more practical fundamentals and, as the world has witnessed, often result in breathtaking failures.

On the personal side, such a grandiose approach has been labeled the "excessiveness" of the Russian man. Instead of earning $500 in one week, he wants to earn $5000 today; instead of one girlfriend, he has three; not just one drink, but a whole bottle. In simple conversation, a foreigner can often sense expansive thinking. Implication and innuendo are uncharacteristic.

Going hand in hand with the generalistic approach is a lack of self-knowledge and less acute critical faculties than the average Westerner. The Soviet system severely punished all critical thinking. In one sense this is a dazzling quality: a Russian judges others by their broad characteristics, not their trivial faults. He also tends not to suffer from self-consciousness. Looked at another way, lack of self-knowledge can be frustrating. If a Russian finds it unnatural to describe strong feelings, common relationship troubles, whether from the wife or the boss, often develop into big problems.

Nationalism. Russians are deeply nationalistic. Once mobilized by a love for Mother Russia, Russians seemed to accomplish superhuman feats. They threw out Napoleon's invading armies in the nineteenth century and kicked out the Nazis during World War II, despite bitter conditions. In Leningrad (now St. Petersburg), the Nazi army set up a blockade around the city, designed to weaken and starve the population so troops could walk in and take over. Nine hundred days later it was the Nazis who were defeated: Citizens of Leningrad had resisted and broken the blockade despite inhuman conditions.

Need for authority. Russia has never been a democracy. More than one thousand years of monarchy and communist dictatorship have conditioned Russians to prefer a life that is unquestionably directed by a fearsome chief. Strong self-reliance and independence are alien to the Russian character. The Russian holds a deep-seated fear of independence and has difficulty making decisions. In the workplace, the boss often must assert his authority to be respected.

Fatalism. Most Russians believe the majority of meaningful events in life are beyond their control, such as difficult situations in the family, the workplace, the government or the world. A fatalistic attitude has been linked to the widespread problem of alcoholism and is believed to encourage submissiveness, especially among women, who readily accept their powerlessness in difficult situations.

Communality. Even before the Soviet Union, Russians were steeped in the communal tradition for centuries. Individual needs and desires are subjugated to the group. Typical Western ideas such as unique self-expression, alternative lifestyles, a sense of private ownership, or individual pay scales are new to Russia.

In the workplace, foreigners notice a marked difference between a Russian working alone within a good infrastructure and a Russian working with other Russians. A Russian alone will often excel. "But when he gets with other Russians, his attitude immediately changes," explains one Russian business consultant who has lived in the U.S. "He tends to lose his seriousness in his approach to work."

Accepting Misfortune

Subjugation to a harsh central authority figure for thousands of years seems to have inculcated in Russians an unchallenged acceptance of misfortune. Russians tend to believe they cannot influence bad things that happen in their lives because all those bad things are as implacable as natural disasters.

Rysazrd Kapuscinski, in his book *Imperium* (Alfred A. Knopf, 1994) explains this point from the perspective of a man who was sentenced to a prison camp:

> The camps belong to the natural order of things, and not to the human order. Can a man rebel against the fact of a great frost or a terrible flood? If a flood comes and someone starts to shake his fist at the river, people will say that he is mad, that he escaped from an insane asylum. If a flood comes, one must climb the highest tree and wait patiently until the water recedes. That is rationality, that is the only reasonable response. If a man finds himself in a camp, he shouldn't revolt, because they will shoot him for that; he should just live in such a way that ensures he will survive. Maybe, sometime the water in the river will recede; maybe, sometime, they will release him from the camp. Nothing more can or even need be done.

Kapuscinski goes on to argue that Russians "accept all misfortunes, even those caused by the soullessness and stupidity of those in power, as the excesses of an omnipotent and capricious nature, on the order of floods, earthquakes or exceptionally cold winters. The thoughtlessness or brutality of authorities is just one of the cataclysms that nature so liberally

dispenses. One must understand this; one must resign oneself
to it."

Broken Generational Bonds

Mikhail Gorbachev's *perestroika* in the 1980s seems to have
snapped the close generational bonds shared by Soviet citizens.
Roughly speaking, those who were born before 1955 remained
more rooted in Soviet tradition. The younger generation
experienced a profoundly different upbringing: living in
chaos, bombarded by foreign influences and ideas, and struggling to be self-sufficient. The old and the young were affected
the most.

In past times, younger people were less impelled to make
money and think about themselves. It was not unusual for
the entire family, including the grandparents, to regularly
come together to eat, work at the *dacha,* travel or visit relatives.
Today, Russian youth are becoming more commercially oriented. Many speak or are studying foreign languages, as they
believe a job with a foreign company offers nice working conditions and security for the future. They sometimes see parents
and older people as "Soviets" in the sense of being inflexible
and rooted in archaic Soviet traditions. Social commentators
mourn that youth are more interested in television than reading; in stretching the law to their advantage rather than helping to create a fundamental system of fair laws; and in ignoring
the government rather than becoming interested in how to
improve it.

Despite changing attitudes, perhaps the most respected figure in Russia is still the grandmother (*babushka*). Her general
character—sensible, gruff, strong, trustworthy—puts her in a
position of authority. She also works physically hard. Her
daily routine includes carrying sacks of food from the market,
climbing stairs and fighting crowds on the transport systems,
cleaning and cooking. She networks with other *babushkas* and
they share information on prices, the neighborhood and family gossip. Often she has a major influence on the affairs of

the children and grandchildren and steps in when family tragedies arise.

For the older people, quick adaptation to fundamental societal changes has brought despair, fear and a yearning for the good old days. Those over age thirty-five tend to have the greatest difficulties in adapting. Financial security is the top concern of the older generation, who have effectively been robbed. One pensioner, for example, bemoans how she invested 1000 roubles in the Russian equivalent of a savings bond in 1980. Back then, the amount was equivalent to more than $1000 at the official exchange rate. She had the idea of cashing the bond in fifteen years and retiring in security. Today her investment is worth 10,000 roubles, which is currently the equivalent of about $2. To compound the problem, the meager pensions don't rise in correlation with inflation.

Relationships with Foreigners

For centuries, Russia has been in conflict between accepting and rejecting the West. The *zapadniks* favor adopting a Western lifestyle while the *slavophiles* fiercely push for an all-Slavic way of life. Then, generations of Russians under Soviet rule were strictly forbidden from contacting any foreigners. Soviet ideology taught that Western ideas, products and people themselves were trying to undermine the stability and sanctity of the USSR.

So thorough was this kind of education, that even today some older Russians have a lingering distrust of foreigners. There's a story of an Irish businesswoman living in Moscow who was harassed by neighbors demanding monthly payments for having to endure living beside a foreigner.

The problem is more complicated since the demise of the USSR. Many Russian politicians, out to ease the pain of a wounded national psyche and advance their careers, try to convince Russians that the West is still out to destroy a vulnerable Russia. Suspicion may prevail even among the sophisticated business circles in large cities like Moscow and St. Petersburg. Sometimes these beliefs are reinforced: It didn't help matters much when the market opened up for foreign products and some companies dumped overruns, outdated food, discontinued products and other inferior goods in Russia.

Also complicating the problem is the huge economic disparity between Russians and foreigners. Because the average Russian earns such a small salary (about $200 per month), nearly all Russians believe foreigners are rich. The wise businessperson should keep gifts inexpensive, behave and dress somewhat modestly and refrain from talking about money or bragging about wealth. Sometimes this is difficult to do since many Russians express a burning curiosity about foreign countries, which they have only seen through foreign television programs. Talk inevitably turns to how foreigners live and Russians think nothing of asking how much a person earns in a year. Prepare some polite answers that sidestep the question.

Most Russians will extend a hearty welcome to foreigners despite decades of indoctrination. Nonetheless, the visiting businessperson should keep the Soviet past in mind, be sensitive and exercise patience.

Discrimination and Racism

It would be nice to say that Russians are grappling with the problem of racism. But the more realistic statement is that shameless racism is widespread and tolerated. Most Russians keep their opinions private. Foreign minority businesspeople, however, should be aware that they will likely be distrusted.

One inflexible issue is the inherent dislike and distrust of people who do not have a Caucasian complexion. Businesspersons who are black or Asian, for example, will be forced to overcome virulent stereotypes of inferiority and dishonesty.

Part of the reason for this goes back to the Russian tendency to blame outsiders for all their problems. Indeed, today certain groups are openly striving for the ethnic purity of Russia, purging it of foreign influence, without much opposition.

Another cause goes back to the USSR's anti-Western propaganda barrage, which portrayed abominable racism as a common occurrence in the West. Soviet school history books, recalls one Russian educator, depicted a black man being burned alive by American racists, labeling it a typical practice. Until the 1990s, most Russians knew nothing about black doctors, astronauts, lawyers, generals or city mayors. From childhood, they absorbed images of blacks unemployed, terrified of police and poverty stricken. Firm stereotypes were formed, labeling blacks as weak, uneducated and poor. As a result, unabashed racism is prevalent. Black foreign businesspeople could be randomly insulted in public, often without ill intent but simply as a matter of habit. Note that the Russian word *nigir* is not intended as an insult, but equates to the English "Negro."

Russians are generally a conservative people, highly intolerant of nonconventional lifestyles, such as homosexuality or mixed marriages, which they consider shocking and decadent. Black men who have white girlfriends or wives and take them out in public will almost certainly attract trouble.

Russians can be staunchly anti-Semitic as well, although they tend to keep their opinions to themselves. A circulating conspiracy theory proposes that the principle actors involved in the Bolshevik Revolution, including Lenin and Trotsky, were Jews who wanted to turn Russia into the new Jewish homeland through the creation of the communist system. A Jewish conspiracy was a handy way to absolve all Russians of responsibility for their own fate.

Russians categorize people by ethnicity, which they refer to as "nationality." The foreigner should know that Russians will invariably want to know a person's last name, where he is from and where his family was from. A name will often tell nationality and Russians strongly believe in generalizations of nationalities, religions and races. The practice is not necessarily malicious, only ingrained.

Attitudes toward minorities are slowly changing since the time Russia opened its doors and embraced new freedoms. But remember that a minority in a big city like Moscow or St.

Petersburg is more common than in a small city or village, where time seems to stand still.

Money and Relationships

In a few short years, money has taken on a new and burning importance in Russia. Before, Russians had virtually no financial worries, while today, money rules lives and in some instances changes people drastically. Therefore, the foreign visitor should be aware that the mere fact of being a foreigner causes virtually all Russians to view him as rich.

Being too generous may quickly lead to exploitation. Russians' salaries are minuscule compared to the average Western salary, so a foreigner will often feel the temptation to absorb all expenses. But a general lack of concern about spending money, even small sums, will set the tone of the relationship. Buying lunch at an extravagant restaurant may not be the best idea. Chances are Russians will continually expect that level of spending in the future, feel uninhibited about asking for more, and perhaps become offended if it is not forthcoming. Years of dependency on a welfare state which provided money without making demands has conditioned the psyche of many Russians. Some are engaged in the search for a replacement *Big Provider* and may look to a foreigner to fulfill that role.

If the Russian sees sensible frugality from the start, the relationship fares better. The foreigner should show concern about all money he must spend and often ask the Russian friend to share in the cost, no matter how small a sum it may seem.

Moreover, foreigners can be grievously overcharged. Two-tier price systems, sanctioned by the government, set higher prices for foreigners in services such as medical care and transportation, supporting the virulent stereotype that all foreigners are rich. Some Russian companies and individuals see the two-tier system as an official policy to overcharge foreigners. The visitor should question all prices that seem out of bounds.

In some cases, a generous person can be swiftly exploited. Foreigners tend to be a transient population and a Russian may figure he will never see the foreigner again. So why not get all that he can now?

Other Russians carry over an admirable trait from the Soviet culture. To accept money for helping, for doing repairs, etc. would be profiteering—something against the ideals of Soviet philosophy. This group would never overcharge anyone and often help others for free.

Friends to Depend On

A good friend is a staple of life, like food. A Russian tends to believe he or she must always have one or two good friends to rely on. While the idea of solid friendships is nothing unusual, Russians differ in that they seldom consider solving their problems themselves, through their own efforts. The best solution is nearly always through the help of others.

The concepts of independence and self-reliance are unfamiliar to most Russians and a possible cause of frustrations for Westerners. Moreover, in comparison to Western families, Russian family members are more strongly dependent on each other. Therefore, Russians may not hesitate to closely involve themselves with other people. They may not worry about how much of the person's time they are taking up, and may not have internal gauges to determine if they are making the relationship too demanding. To Westerners, especially Americans, the Russian friend may seem to become dependent, both financially and emotionally.

The Importance of Wasting Time

A particular beauty of Russians is their innate desire to enjoy natural pleasures of life, a vanishing quality that tends to be neutralized in people from free market economies. Wasting time is one way in which they remind themselves that life is more than a series of goals and results spiced with numbers.

Wasting time with a friend is central to the Russian notion of friendship. Time-conscious foreigners will feel anxious doing nothing. But the importance of wasting time should not be ignored.

Time is wasted (in small amounts, of course) on the job as a fifteen-minute coffee break and chat regularly extends to half an hour. It is wasted by habitually visiting Russians in their apartments, joking and drinking, and inviting them into the home to do the same. It is also wonderfully wasted at a marathon dinner without an agenda or time constraints.

Listmakers and workaholics will despair in Russia.

Sharing

Four Russian friends meet. One has a chocolate bar. He pulls out his pocket knife and carefully cuts the chocolate into four minuscule but equal pieces and divides it among the four. In other countries, four friends would not typically think of equally distributing such a small portion. "If I want one, I will buy my own" would perhaps be the attitude. In Russia, the sharing of food or consumables is of primary importance.

The foreigner witnessing Russian friends drinking beer together will likely see a similar ritual. One bottle is opened, and it fills all glasses. When that's finished, one more bottle is opened and it fills all glasses. The process continues in this way. Therefore, when eating, drinking or smoking, always first offer Russian friends the same. It is necessary to insist two or three times because the Russian typically will refuse out of politeness. Not offering to share could be considered a slight, but for more expensive things, make it clear beforehand that the cost will be shared.

Politeness

Russians tend to be unusually polite, depending of course, on the level of education and breeding. Men open doors for women, light their cigarettes, and help them off buses. Friends often shake hands each time they come and go. All strangers, older people and authority figures are addressed as *vui* (the formal you). The informal you, *ti*, is used for close friends, children and immediate family.

Public Etiquette

Some general rules of public conduct apply. In Russia, pointing at a person is considered rude. The visitor should try not to sit with legs by resting an ankle on the knee, especially around old people, as it's considered a hostile assertion of oneself. When visiting a Russian Orthodox church, women should cover their heads and wear a skirt and men should not wear hats.

Independent Western women often clash with Russian men. The Russian man gets insulted if the woman uncorks the wine bottle, opens the door for a man, lights a cigarette herself, carries a heavy shopping bag when walking with a man or pays for a date.

Russians have many peculiar public customs they abide by. For example, if a Russian accidentally steps on someone's foot, the Russian may insist that that person step on his foot; if this bilateral foot-stepping ritual is not carried out, it is believed that the next time the two parties meet there will be an argument. These strange customs vary by region and are more common among the older generation.

When meeting a Russian acquaintance, always allow thirty minutes if the person is late. Difficulties with transport, great distances and a casual attitude toward timeliness will interfere with punctuality. If by chance a foreigner meets a Russian friend on the street, he should always stop to chat for a minute. Don't just say hello and walk by. Remove a glove when shaking hands. All handshakes should be firm, and always inquire about family members before talking about yourself or business. For example, "How is Elena Alexandrovna?" If the foreigner is acquainted with his friend's family, he can ask the friend to "pass a hello" to the wife and children. Never be too busy to acknowledge your Russian friend, because in Russia, relationships come before time commitments.

As a rule, anytime a visitor is invited to an apartment, he should bring some modest gifts. A bottle of wine for the host, perhaps flowers for the woman of the house (always in odd numbered lots) and maybe chocolate for the children. It's perfectly acceptable for a male to present flowers to the wife of a Russian man. Gifts are a central part of Russian relationships. Russians value gifts because they show that the giftgiver is thinking about them. Being late seems to be habitual with Russians, but rarely is anyone ever late for a dinner party, as this will offend the woman who has worked hard to prepare the food.

When arriving at or leaving a restaurant, party, office or friend's home, always make sure that all Russian friends receive a personal "hello" or "good-bye." Forgetting this simple etiquette can offend Russians.

Closed Today

Government, banks and most businesses may shut down for lengthy periods during the holidays. The majority of Russians celebrate December 31 and January 1 (*Novy Gode*) on the same level as Westerners celebrate Christmas Eve and Christmas Day. On December 31, the entire family has a big dinner together and exchanges gifts. It's also a time to call friends and patch up any festering disagreements. Later that night, the young people go to their friends' homes for parties and traditionally stay out all night. There is even a Santa Claus equivalent—*Dyet Maross* ("Grandfather Frost") who brings good children presents on December 31.

The Orthodox Christmas and New Year are celebrated on January 2 and January 7 respectively. Therefore, foreigners should be aware that most of Russia shuts down from the end of December to the middle of January, much as Asia slows down for some weeks during the Chinese New Year in February. Summer is also a difficult time to find key Russians in business and government, as most take four to six weeks and relax at their *dachas* in the countryside.

Another important holiday is Women's Day on March 8, a day in honor of women. On this work holiday, all women are doted on by men.

Even when no holidays are on the calendar, finding people in their offices can be difficult. Phone calls are generally not returned quickly. If unsuccessful in reaching the person by phone after several tries, it may be necessary for someone to visit the office in person and leave a message.

Superstitions

Religion was suppressed and discredited during the seventy years of Soviet rule. The generation of Russians that have grown up without belief in a supreme being have also lost their faith in the substitute god of communism. As a result, a spiritual vacuum exists. Many Russians are firm believers in astrology, while others abide by ancient pagan superstitions.

A visitor to Russia may be astonished by their superstitions. The country's brilliant scientists engineered and launched the world's only orbiting space station, *Mir*. But in everyday life, a taxi driver could throw out his passengers and swerve into the opposite direction if a black cat crosses in front of his cab. It happens. Russians may joke about their superstitions, but they take them seriously.

Extend your hand to shake as you enter the doorway of a host's apartment and he only smiles sheepishly, refusing to shake hands across a doorway because it's bad luck. A waitress in a restaurant accidentally spills a salt shaker and tables of jaded diners begin throwing three dashes of salt over their left shoulders then spitting three times to ward off evil spirits. (Many Russians believe a devil sits on your left shoulder, an angel sits on your right.)

Don't leave an empty bottle on the table because it could mean depleted food resources, and don't whistle indoors because your money will fly out the window. Pouring a bottle backhanded is not only rude, but it means your money will dwindle away, and sitting at the corner of a table means a single person will remain single for seven years.

Many omens prevail: If a knife falls from the table, a man will soon visit; if a fork falls, a female will arrive; if someone coughs while eating at the dinner table, a man will arrive very quickly; before embarking on a journey, the travelers and everyone in the house should sit down for thirty seconds before exiting to ensure safe passage; and a person leaving the home should never go back to retrieve something he has forgotten—it's bad luck. If it's crucial to go back and take the forgotten item, he should spit over the left shoulder three times, look in a mirror and smile.

Also, the number "3" holds great significance for Russians, going back to Orthodox traditions of the Holy Trinity. When someone gives flowers, they typically give three. Flowers in even-numbered lots are for funerals only. Don't make that mistake!

The Culture of Drinking

The average Russian has a high tolerance for alcohol and can drink the average foreigner under the table. Refusing a drink can be misinterpreted as an offense to the host and is a serious breach of etiquette. The visitor should be prepared to drink one or two small doses of vodka. Russians will pressure guests to continue drinking. Once a bottle is opened, Russians like to say, it must be finished.

At all dinner parties there will be loads of alcohol. Russians tend to drink large quantities consistently but slowly and always in combination with *zakuski* or snacks. They tend not to mix their drinks with juices but drink strong alcohol straight. Gushing toasts honoring guests will be used as frequent excuses to raise the shot glass to the mouth. The visitor is advised to have some excuse to weasel out of excessive drinking. For example, religion forbids imbibing; current medication prohibits alcohol drinking; driving will be necessary later on.

Being late to a birthday party sometimes obligates the tardy person to drink a so-called penalty drink, a tall glass of straight vodka. Refusing will only bring insistent demands to drink.

The Mystique of Vodka

In Russia, vodka is an old friend, good company, an expected guest at any celebration—and the target of blame when something bad happens. Vodka's mystique extends to the field of medicine, where its healing powers are legend. Many Russians swear that a cure for the common cold is a shot of vodka with pepper added. Russians also use small amounts of a type of herbal vodka (*Balsam*) to bring relief from sinus or gastrointestinal disorders, influenza, headaches or just a plain old bad mood.

Vodka is drunk straight and always accompanied by snacks such as salmon, caviar, cucumbers, mushrooms, potatoes, onions, herring, cucumbers and bread.

Vodka's history in Russia goes back to the fifteenth century, when Russians first mass produced an alcohol-and-water mixture for export which they named *vodka*, a form of the word *voda* (water) that refers to pure glacial water—without minerals. Vodka enjoyed a special status among Russians. Unlike beer, vodka could be sipped by farmers toiling in the fields to keep warm. A small quantity carried the wallop preferred by the hearty outdoor working men. Russian monarchies popularized vodka by giving it pride of place at the czar's dinner table. Acceptance by the elite changed vodka from a crude country brew into an endearing national symbol.

Russians drink vodka mainly with guests after the finish of the work week, to relax at the *dacha* or at the *banya* (public bath). The ritual of drinking vodka can be opulent and rife with symbolic meaning. At a funeral vodka will likely be drunk by the bereaved family at the moment following the deceased's burial. When Russians share a little vodka with a new acquaintance, the gesture can represent efforts to smooth the transition from stranger to friend. If a foreigner refuses, mistrust may form. Foreign guests invited into Russian homes and offered a small glass should try not to refuse. But expect pressure to drink excessively and prepare excuses to avoid getting plastered.

Vodka has been blamed for everything from failed marriages to the collapse of the USSR. Indeed, alcoholism has been Russia's main social problem for decades. During *perestroika*, Mikhail Gorbachev tried to curtail alcoholism by restricting the sale of vodka and launching a national anti-alcohol education campaign. It failed, and vodka was soon freely sold again, amid the rambunctious cheers of the male population.

The Banya

Russians believe in combating minor illnesses, a hangover or a nagging bad mood with a visit to the *banya*, or public bath, which includes a hot room or *parilka*.

Banya—or the concept of the steam room or sauna—have existed in Russia for well over 1,000 years. But during Soviet times, huge aristocratic apartments in Moscow and St. Petersburg were divided in order to become communal apartments with one family per room, all sharing a kitchen and toilet but lacking shower facilities. Many more were built to provide a public place where such families could get clean. Fathers bring their sons to the men's *banya* and grandmothers bring their granddaughters to the women's *banya*. Local companies also installed their own *banya*—*vedomstvennie banya*—on the premises to serve the workers.

Good health begins with a good beating. Russians typically bring a *vyenik* (small tree branch) to the steam room and beat the body with it to open the pores of the skin, promoting sweat. *Vyenike* can be from birch, oak or eucalyptus trees—each offering its own natural scent.

The branch is first doused in cold water, then left in hot water for a few minutes to soften it. Variations on the proper use of a *vyenik* exist. One common method is to lie down on the bench in the steam room, developing a sweat. A friend takes the *vyenik* (sometimes two—one in each hand) and begins a light dusting movement from the toes to the head and back, which soon turns into a thrashing, creating a massage effect.

The *parilka* is hot—more than 110° Fahrenheit—making the branch hot in a bare hand. Also, any movement involves air friction, delivering even hotter blasts of wind that can singe the hair. Many *vyenik* enthusiasts wear gloves and a wool hat inside the steam room. The thrashing, Russians believe, not only opens the pores but promotes healing and many people work on areas of the body that are sore.

After the steam room, some people will quickly plunge into a nearby chilly 35° Fahrenheit tub of water. Quite a few Russians believe quick, extreme temperature changes bring health benefits. They claim blood flow speeds up, cleaning the veins of cholesterol and hastening the body's healing process.

Over the years, the *banya* developed into a place for socializing. Sitting naked in the *parilka* and chatting with strangers seems to detoxify not only the body but also psychological stress. In the changing room, eating and drinking are allowed and beer and vodka are for sale. Small *banyi* parties are typical, and old Communist Party officials met regularly in the *banya*. Soldiers on a weekend pass may spend hours together there, drinking and talking. A neighborly atmosphere prevails that can seldom be found elsewhere.

Cautious Communication

Because of their Soviet past, Russians have peculiarities of communication. The Soviet government ruled by fear of authority, affecting all aspects of life including language. For decades it was forbidden for strangers to gather in groups and talk on the street. Moreover, if one stranger said something politically incorrect to another stranger, the police could be summoned. Sometimes friends denounced friends, wives turned in husbands, and colleagues pointed fingers at each other. KGB agents surveilled the undesirables and often hauled them away to prison. On the job, in official clubs, in the shops, a Soviet citizen was better off speaking as little as possible—and then carefully selecting his words.

Only in the 1980s during *perestroika* were people able to gather publicly and voice their opinions without fear of certain reprisal. Therefore, there is no tradition in large Russian cities of smiling at strangers, chance meetings or unsolicited help. Should a visitor attempt to make small talk with a stranger, the stranger will likely walk away. If a woman smiles or makes eye contact with a male stranger, it will likely be misinterpreted as an invitation.

Today, Russians speak in neutral and general terms. The question "What did you do last night?" would likely be answered by an American with a detailed description of where he went, what he did, how much he spent and what he thought. In Russia, the answer will be something like "I was busy." Similarly, "Where do you work?" may be answered by "At a trading company." Such talk is a protective measure; the person is cautious about revealing any detailed information. Unfortunately, foreigners often misinterpret the generic answers as curt retorts.

Feelings Before Logic

Russia's business relationships can be confusing for foreigners. Western businesspeople tend to follow logic and cast feelings aside when entering into a business relationship. But Russians tend to follow feeling and hold logic at bay. Formal contracts don't mean as much as an affirmation of a feeling about another.

Business deals in some fast-track sectors in Moscow may be quick and impersonal. In other cities, such as St. Petersburg, establishing a personal relationship with a business acquaintance is the preferred procedure.

Russians tend not to do business over the telephone. During Soviet times, big business deals were often made in the sauna, with vodka, smoked fish and caviar nearby. Today, before major decisions are made, a Russian sometimes likes to invite a foreign businessperson to a restaurant or perhaps into the home, where he introduces his family and enjoys a meal and drinks with good conversation. Business talk comes later. The foreigner who wants to "get down to nuts and bolts" quickly may be distrusted. Let the Russian decide if and when business topics should be discussed at the informal meeting.

Foreign businesspeople like results. They value efficiency and don't like to waste time with formalities. Russians, though, generally have a particular interest in becoming personally acquainted with the people with whom they deal. Try not to hurry things along.

The tone of a relationship is often set at the first informal meeting, and its importance is worth stressing. A Russian probably won't ask a foreigner where he studied, nor assess his credentials, test his business knowledge or be strongly interested in other quantitative information to form a character judgment.

The following are a few criteria by which a Russian forms a judgment about a foreigner:

A genuine appreciation of some aspects of Russia. Everyone appreciates some aspect of Russia, even if they dislike the country as a whole. Voicing praise about Russia in an educated and heartfelt manner touches the average Russian. Inquiring about Russia in a noncritical way is also pleasing.

A sense of humor. Nearly all Russians thoroughly enjoy anecdotes and humorous rejoinders. It doesn't take much to score laughs. But try to be familiar with the Russian sense of humor first. So-called one-liners seem to work in both Russia and the West. Humor laced with subtle irony, however, doesn't seem to work well.

Exuberance. Russians build trust with a person who displays a reasonable lack of inhibition. A person with a desire to dance, laugh, drink and express himself is seen as good company. The nervous or jaded person may be hiding something.

Conversation. The visitor who sits modest and silent is at a disadvantage. Russians generally love to converse on nearly any topic and are often impressed by someone displaying an authentic sense of inquisitiveness, a breadth of knowledge or novel ideas. A favorite topic is "How is life different in your country?" The foreigner who can go beyond the superficial and relate some fascinating cultural differences is remembered.

Politeness. Foreigners should respect Russia, older people, the host and his family. Visitors who show an ongoing, genuine interest in the host and his family are well liked. Visitors should also consider well-placed compliments of abilities, such as cooking or singing. But praising an object in a host's home may make him feel obligated to give it to the visitor. Finally, be sincere; Russians tend to recognize insincerity.

A Russian will often use social meetings to get a feel for his guest. If he has a good feeling, the future relationship is tightly secure. The Russian man generally believes the initial sense of a person is the truth—and he's not likely to change his judgment. If the Russian has a bad feeling about his guest, he may still do business with that person but the bond will undoubtedly cause future problems and the partnership, if formed, will be endangered.

When the visitor leaves, he shouldn't set the time for a business meeting in the future. That can be done with a phone call during business hours.

6

DOING BUSINESS IN THE WILD EAST
Emerging Russia

Two Big Cities

Russia's largest patches of economic development include the Far East, where investment from Japan and Asian countries has flowed into small but burgeoning business cities such as Nokhotka and Vladivostok; the Tyumen and Komi Republics (Northwest Russia) where foreign oil companies have set up, creating a modest economic boom; and the Moscow and St. Petersburg regions, which have been flooded by foreign goods and services.

But political power and foreign business is concentrated in Russia's two largest cities, Moscow, with a population of about eight million, and St. Petersburg, with about five million. (Some fifteen other Russian cities, all with populations between 1 and 1.5 million, vie for third place.)

The bulk of foreigners doing business in Russia will concentrate their efforts in one or both of the two largest cities. Outside Russia's two largest cities, the visitor encounters plenty of vestiges from Soviet times. For example, in thriving Moscow, one can find a wide variety of foreign products and services, from McDonald's Restaurants to American Express; by contrast in Novosibirsk, with a population of about 1.2 million, scant foreign businesses are present and relatively few people speak a foreign language.

Moscow and St. Petersburg differ significantly. Historically, Moscow has been heavily influenced by the Mongol empire and traditionally hostile toward Europe. Western Russia (specifically Novgorod and Pskov, two small cities a little south of

St. Petersburg) was steeped in democratic traditions and held strong connections to Europe.

Today Moscow is a melting pot of nationalities and religions, with people from all over the former USSR, including the Central Asian Republics, the Far East, the Siberian North, the Middle East and the Baltic States. In addition, unofficial estimates put Moscow's foreign (mainly Western) population at 100,000—the largest in Russia.

As the capital city and seat of the government, Moscow functions as Russia's power center, although the Kremlin is steadily losing influence in far-flung cities such as Vladivostok. Virtually all the influential decisions and lucrative deals originate in Moscow. By some estimates, 80 percent of all foreign money in Russia is concentrated there. The city's infrastructure is the most advanced and its atmosphere the most commercial in all of Russia. Another distinction is its status as one of the most expensive cities in the world.

St. Petersburg (formerly called Leningrad, Petrograd, and its founding name St. Petersburg) was the capital of Russia until Lenin made Moscow the capital in 1918. The Communists believed it was too close to Europe: Invading armies and Western ideas could too easily infiltrate Russia if her capital was near the Western border.

St. Petersburg can be described more like a big village, with a main street (*Nevsky Prospect*) running through the city center. Despite significant foreign investment, it has a slower commercial pace than Moscow. Throughout its history, St. Petersburg distinguished itself as a cultural and intellectual center. Peter the Great invited European architects and engineers to help build the city. Dostoyevsky and Pushkin lived and wrote great literature there. Music, ballet, architecture, and theater have also shaped the city's character. Moreover, much of Soviet Russia's high-level technological research was done in or around St. Petersburg.

The port city, a few hours from Finland, is also more European-oriented than Moscow, as it has a history of inviting foreigners in to play a part in its growth. Moscow, by contrast, was the city of suspicion and serious politics. Even today, foreign businesspeople say more centralization and bureaucracy exist in Moscow than in St. Petersburg. Stability differs as well. In October 1993, when tank battles raged in Moscow, St. Petersburg remained calm.

Russia's Heavy Industry

Iron and steel production was the driving force behind Soviet modernization, which shaped industry after World War II. Today, basic raw materials form the backbone of industrial exports due to the poor quality of manufactured products, when measured by international standards. Russia's main manufacturing industries are crude steel; cars and trucks; aircraft; chemicals and fertilizers; plastics; cement and building materials; and paper.

Cities were sometimes built around huge industrial complexes that supported the local population. In many cases one plant became the sole producer of a product for the entire USSR. As a result of this practice, numerous monopolies were created throughout the country. An antimonopoly committee with legal backing was formed in the 1990s to monitor monopolistic activities.

Industry tends to be highly labor intensive due to the lack of development of advanced equipment. Most manufacturers are vertically integrated: They manufacture all products and components themselves or their affiliates do.

Industry as a whole is in decline due to inefficient, outdated methods and machinery, worker apathy and lack of cash. Production in many sectors is still falling. Quite a few enterprises are technically bankrupt, although they have been kept alive by low-interest loans received from the state that have little penalty for nonrepayment. Such handouts have removed incentives for failing industries to reorient themselves to new economic conditions.

Moscow is trying to remedy industry through tougher bankruptcy laws and by pushing privatization. The Kremlin put strong emphasis on development of the consumer goods sector (particularly food processing) to address the countrywide product shortages and reduce dependency on imports. So-called defense conversion—transforming a tank factory into a car factory, for example—has been supported by international aid groups. Defense conversion also aims to help Russia's technical wizards design a state-of-the-art CD player rather than focus entirely on improving missile guidance systems.

Want to Buy a Telephone?

It was pay day. But the workers at a large St. Petersburg electronics company hadn't received their salary in months. Because the financially strapped government didn't pay the company for state product orders, the company in turn couldn't pay their employees. Management, under pressure from employees, didn't want to suspend pay for a third month so they paid wages in the product they manufactured—telephones. Employees grudgingly accepted the offer. In these hard economic times, they assumed it was the best compensation they would get. Mrs. M brought home 175 push-button phones in several colors. They sit in her closet. She tries to sell them to wholesalers, shops and friends.

Large factories which employ the bulk of Russia's workforce teeter on the edge of bankruptcy and state employees fear their jobs will soon be lost. Candy, milk, clothes and machinery have all been given in lieu of pay. Employees are often sent on half-paid leave, and some don't bother to go to work at all, but remain a registered employee in case management can pay salary. Typically, employees find other work, perhaps as a secretary at a small firm or selling toys on the street and just occasionally appear at their jobs. In some cases, people actually work full time at a private firm yet maintain their employment at the state factory and collect two salaries.

Russia's numerous factories have few options. Either they wait for government product orders and payment, declare bankruptcy or aggressively seek foreign investors. Dealing with a cash-strapped state and unskilled in marketing, the majority of factories face inevitable bankruptcy. The state continues to subsidize many enterprises to avoid mass unemployment and the possibility of civil disorder. Many of these behemoth factories will keep receiving minimal subsidies so that the average worker collects a tiny wage, which dwindles in value as the rouble devalues.

Ukraine and Belarus

Ukraine and Belarus have large Slavic populations and in many ways they are nearly indistinguishable from Russia. Yet since December 1991, both have been independent countries with control over their own politics and economies. The truck traveling from Moscow to Kiev to Minsk will be crossing two borders. The foreign company selling products in these three countries will be working in three different currencies.

Belarus (Byelorussia, meaning "White Russia") is an agricultural country, with the bulk of the workforce being peasant farmers. In the past it has been a major supplier of food to Russia. Belarus has its own language that differs slightly from Russian in speech and writing, though both sides can understand each other. The Belarus language is still preserved in villages and is used in Minsk.

Likewise, Ukraine has its own language, slightly different from its neighbors, but still understood by them. Despite traditionally close ties to Russians (the beginnings of the Russian state can be traced back to Kiev), Ukrainians feel they are a unique people differing in mentality from their Slavic brothers. (Russians quickly identify Ukrainians by hearing the family name, which typically ends in -*enko* for a man and -*enka* for a woman.) A congenial rivalry has existed between the two, and it seldom has been labeled as serious.

In general, warm relations have existed between the three countries. Despite independence, their shared Slavic culture is expected to strengthen economic and political ties. Moreover, these countries have been increasingly frank in their wish to establish economic integration with Russia, and have come to understand that without Russia's energy supplies they will fall behind a Russia that has already surged ahead of all former republics except the Baltic States. Only Kazakhstan, Turkmenistan and Azerbaijan have their own energy reserves and therefore have the potential for economic independence from Moscow.

Government

Russia's contemporary statehood began in December 1991 with the formation of the Commonwealth of Independent States. Since then, the government has been struggling to transform the giant country into a constitutional state based on the rule of law. Russia's transition seems to inch ahead, fall back, then drift.

The need for a new Russian constitution was approved by the public in an April 1993 referendum. But the communist-era parliament and President Yeltsin argued and brawled over the issue. The parliament held that the country already had a legal constitution which could not simply be swept aside, while Yeltsin maintained that the public referendum gave him the right to do just that. In October 1993 the argument erupted in violence in Moscow when Yeltsin disbanded the parliament and imposed presidential rule. Parliament members refused to budge and tanks were sent in to shell the building and uproot them.

After the smoke cleared, Yeltsin demanded new countrywide elections and a referendum for approval of a new constitution. A new constitution with similarities to the U.S. or French model was approved, providing the office of president with more authority than the parliament. The Russian president serves as head of state, commander in chief of the armed forces and chairman of the Security Council. He has extensive powers of appointment and authority to issue decrees independent of parliament and may also dissolve parliament under special conditions.

The new parliament is made up of a directly elected 450-seat lower house (State Duma) and a 178-seat upper house (Federation Council). Duma members are elected to a four-year term. The Federation Council consists of two representatives from each unit of the Russian Federation serving for two years. Both houses may initiate laws and both bear responsibilities for laws on the budget, federal taxes and other financial policies, but before these laws can be debated in parliament, the right to debate them must first be agreed upon by the whole government. This is intended to ensure that parliament is most effective when working with the government.

Trust in the Government

Relaxing at home, a Russian man turns on the television and hears the government announce that in a few days, only rouble notes printed during the current year will be accepted as valid. The man keeps his rouble savings at home and after some quick checking finds that most of his cash will be worthless. Later television reports try to assuage public panic by explaining that a small amount of old cash may be exchanged immediately for new notes. The rest of the old notes may be exchanged only if they are deposited in a bank for six months. (In those six months the rouble drops 50 perecnt in value).

Such was the situation faced by Russians one day in July of 1993. The declaration hurt many families. But a situation in which Russians are dealt a devastating blow by their leaders is by no means unusual.

Trust in the government is low. Falling living standards are largely behind the decline. Politicians are held in low esteem and the political process is treated with skepticism and cynicism. Today's Russians do not believe that exercising their new right to vote will improve their lives. An extraordinary series of city elections in St. Petersburg in 1994 saw not one candidate elected from hundreds of aspirants to office because not enough people showed up at polling booths—even though election day was extended twenty-four hours. A second election soon after did not fare much better, and for months the city had no elected government.

Of course, deception has been a core operating principle of Russia's leaders throughout history. After the Revolution of 1917, many Russians truly believed in the promise of a future communist paradise when life would be bliss. Some Soviet citizens even named their children after persons or symbols of the new Soviet state—Stalinina, Oktyabrina, Trac-tora, Kolhoza—believing that they would become citizens of the promised utopia. Severe hardship and even death were easier to endure, as they were deemed necessary to reach the glorious future.

Russians' vital sacrifices for their leaders have usually been made without question. Today, the key element missing is that Russia's leaders cannot confidently assert a promise of future prosperity which anyone would believe in. Sacrifices, many feel, are made for nothing. Citizens today can also openly voice their dissatisfaction without fear of retribution, which tends to promote an infectious cynicism whenever policies or solutions are advanced.

But in spite of open bitterness and loathing for many of their politicians, people sometimes show an almost childlike faith in the government's ability to help them. For instance, despite numerous well-publicized cases of dubious investment schemes going bust without government intervention, many people still invest, refusing to believe their government will allow it to happen once again. The notion of personal responsibility is not highly developed. The Soviet Big Brother had its benevolent side—cradle-to-the-grave health care, education, employment, pensions and more. Russians became accustomed to being cared for, and letting go of that attachment will take time and inner strength.

Distrust, though, should not be equated with eroding patriotism. Despite strong public cynicism toward those in charge, nearly every Russian remains deeply patriotic—an apparently ingrained quality. A Russian joke popular in the early 1980s illustrates the extent of patriotism:

During bad economic times, a foreigner came to Russia and took a prostitute. When they finished, he asked if she wanted to be paid in dollars, which were very valuable at the time.

"No," she answered.

"In what way can I pay you?"

"Take your missiles out of Western Europe!"

Businessmen and Society

Russians often speak of business and crime as if they were synonyms. *Beeznismyeni* has entered the Russian language and is usually used in a sneering way, spoken as an insult. Tax evasion, extortion and contract murders are visible realities of today's business climate, severely tainting the reputation of Russian businesspeople. Foreign businesspeople fare better, but entrepreneurs and small company owners may be considered shifty. Consider that the majority of foreign businesspeople attracted to Russia are characteristically short-term thinkers who take high risks in hopes of earning a quick fortune.

Several factors complicate the issue: There is no concept of a social contract between business and society, business ethics were never taught in Russia, and to Russians, a truly weird notion is that of the socially responsible company giving monetary gifts to universities or hospitals or otherwise investing in society.

Further, Russia's two predominant business cultures are at odds with each other. Employees of the old Soviet structure work at factories and state-run businesses and live in fear of losing their jobs. Many are older than forty and have held the same job their whole lives—the factory is much like their home. They fear privitization and foreign management, aware that staff will inevitably be trimmed, and the purchase of a newly privatized business often spreads an atmosphere of distrust and resentment among the employees.

Also, Russia is a nation where the phrase "capitalist sharks" was used until recently to describe anyone who aspired to more than a locally made Lada car and a grim concrete box apartment. Russians were taught for decades that a person with more than others was to be despised. The disgusted cry of *speculant!* can still be heard when prices are senselessly raised by ambitious entrepreneurs. (Until a few short years ago, buying from one place and selling at a higher price in another was considered "speculation," punishable by a mandatory two-year sentence).

Old attitudes linger. Even educated, English-speaking Russians who have traveled abroad can harbor prejudices about the character of people engaged in business. Ordinary people may still fail to understand why a store can be allowed to sell the same goods at a higher price than a neighboring store.

Banks and Companies: A Stormy Relationship

Payday is an adventure for many company accountants. On payday, an accountant may arrive at a bank with a small plastic bag and stuff it with tens of millions of roubles withdrawn from the company account. The accountant then cautiously carries the money back to the firm and dishes out stacks of roubles for the payroll. Some banks are starting to provide armored car delivery service for payroll, but the general practice of carrying large amounts of money throughout the city is illustrative of a banking infrastructure that is still busy evolving. In fact, many foreigners cite the banking infrastructure as one of the chief obstacles to doing business in Russia.

Russia's complex, unpredictable banking regulations, many of which are intended to fight illegal activities, restrict efficiency and create constant headaches. Foreign businesspeople complain that regulations are numerous, unclear and contradictory. Moreover, the Central Bank can, in principle, confiscate all money from transactions it deems illegal.

Daily company transactions can be arduous and complicated. There are no checks. Credit and debit cards are entering the scene, but their use is limited. Even though payrolls are settled in cash, it is not possible to withdraw money to pay even small bills. Almost every legal company-to-company transaction in Russia takes place by bank transfer.

Yet the phrase *domestic money transfer* can rattle even seasoned foreign businesspeople. Surprisingly, international transfers are often less problematic than domestic ones since Russia has no electronic bank payment system within its borders. Paperwork is still carried by couriers or sent by the notoriously slow Russian post. Domestic transfers, even within the same region, are supposed to be completed within three working days, but often the money arrives much later, and the receiving company loses if the rouble has lost value.

Each transfer must be signed by the company director and chief accountant. (A common tactic for delaying bill payment is to say the director or accountant is absent.) When a transfer is registered at the bank, a payment number is received. Some foreigners say banks demand lengthy, detailed contract information on a simple transfer of money, unnecessarily prying into the affairs of private businesses.

Banks are set up in a wheel shape for each of the many regions within Russia. At the center of each region is a branch of the Central Bank of Russia. On the outer points of the wheel spokes are the local banks. Any money transfers follow a specific procedure, going from the local bank to the branch of the Central Bank in one region, to the branch of the Central Bank in another region—or hub to hub, going by the wheel analogy.

After arriving at the hub, the money is sent down the correct spoke to the destination bank. Officially, for each "hub-to-hub" transfer, three days are allowed. But, for instance, from St. Petersburg to Vladivostok, five Central Bank branches (or five hubs) are involved. In addition, for travel between the hub and a local bank, one to two days are allowed.

In principle it sounds somewhat reasonable. But the hubs often "lose" the documents which accompany the money in the transfer—then "find" them again in several weeks. During the delay the Central Bank branch could likely be loaning or investing the money in currencies or stock markets. Because of the rouble's tendency toward steady devaluation, problems result when the delay is too long.

The Rebirth of Banking

Russia's banking industry is composed chiefly of three types of banks: those formerly state owned, those founded from scratch after a 1988 decree, and those founded by state enterprises. The Central Bank of Russia, located in Moscow, rules over all the country's banks. Foreign banks have opened representative offices in Moscow and St. Petersburg but by order of a presidential decree only a few are licenses to serve Russian customers. The result? Lack of competition preserved a sluggishness. Without being bettered by Western banks, Russian banks have little incentive to improve service and infrastructure.

Lack of ordinary Western banking services severely obstructs the development of the small and midsize business sectors. Russian banks want the big customers, such as city government pension funds or the payrolls for state enterprises, and believe smaller businesses are not worth the trouble. Interest on loans has reached three digits, and often fees in the thousands of dollars are required just to open an account. Individual checking accounts don't exist. Even simple services such as money exchanging and check cashing entail long, frustrating procedures. Many banks don't have computers, yet even if a bank has a hundred computers, they probably aren't part of a network, thereby slowing all transactions.

Struggling to get on its feet, the banking industry developed many internal problems. In the former USSR, banks doled out money to state enterprises in accordance with state-approved plans, so the borrower's ability to repay was not an issue. Stephen Uuley, who works for accountants Ernst and Young in St. Petersburg, points out that credit appraisal skills were not developed during Soviet times. As a result, credit risk is an especially serious problem for Russia's banks. Bank employees must learn to identify enterprises with potential for growth which can bear the higher interest costs if their loans are to be repaid. A defaulted loan or two may cause the bank to collapse.

Many banks are also infiltrated by organized crime. Russian bankers can find themselves the targets of special attention. A spate of slayings of bank managers in 1993 and 1994, especially in Moscow, has roused banks into taking strict security measures.

Bankers are usually killed when they won't cooperate with criminal groups in the running of their banks. Criminals are switching from brute force to refined attempts to undermine banks' economic security, as they now prefer coming through the boardroom door with a briefcase, rather than coming through the front door with automatic weapons. Organized crime groups, who make fortunes in various trading and commodity rackets, can also afford to buy controlling shares in banks to attain a direct say in their policies. In turn, such economic security problems lead to personal safety problems for honest bankers who are then forced to cooperate.

No doubt, problems exist. But the steady introduction of modern technology and staff retraining is prodding development. U.S.-based technology company Andrew Corporation installed an optical fiber network through Moscow and St. Petersburg subway tunnels, then linked the two cities by running fiber optic cable along the railroad tracks. The system serves as a link to telecommunications companies and offers a state-of-the-art alternative to the antiquated local phone system. Bank branches and stock markets can be linked for instant, secure communication.

Insiders recommend keeping an eye on St. Petersburg to gauge the health of Russia's banking industry. Pre-Revolutionary St. Petersburg was a major European banking center with a stock market on par with London and New York. Industry insiders believe St. Petersburg will regain its former status and even surpass Moscow as Russia's financial center. As early as 1990, St. Petersburg had only a half-dozen banks. Each catered to a specific industry and was run by the state. Today, the city boasts more than seventy private banks, including two with 100 percent foreign capital—Credit Lyonnais and BNP-Dresdner.

Stock Markets

Russia established its first stock market at the end of the nineteenth century in St. Petersburg. After the Revolution, Lenin's New Economic Policy allowed the stock market to thrive from 1921 through 1928, until Stalin's reforms dissolved the bourse.

Today Russia has several stock markets in St. Petersburg and Moscow. Investment in potentially prosperous oil and mining industries can be handsomely rewarding to bold investors. Foreign brokerages have set up in Moscow to accommodate demand. Moreover, Russia sorely needs foreign investment to continue its reforms.

But the nascent stock markets should be approached with caution. Currently there are no capital markets laws defining the rights of shareholders and stories of abuse have been well publicized: Directors of a Russian enterprise called a shareholder meeting without telling shareholders and proceeded to ban all trading of company shares; a massive oil company issued millions of extra shares without telling investors, raising the question of who owns what percentage; and a Russian company sold millions of dollars of its shares to a foreign investor, then scratched the investor's name off the company register—which legally renders the shares worthless. The money paid for the shares was lost.

Trading of some listed companies is based mainly on speculation. In some instances, stock prices rise in companies which have accrued massive debt and may be living off government credits. Buying is usually based on rumor and few care to examine financial possibilities. Price to earnings ratios can vary dramatically.

Foreign investors will remain justifiably nervous until Russia's Securities Exchange Commission assumes tighter control. The Commission has received foreign technical help to modernize and curtail shareholder abuses.

Intellectual Property

The idea was potentially lucrative: Translate English language novels into Russian and sell them countrywide. Russians are voracious readers and few translated modern Western classics were in the bookshops. A Western entrepreneur secured the rights and hired a team to translate three novels into Russian. The finished manuscripts were delivered to the printer, who promised to complete a large print run by a specific date.

When the day arrived, the printer said there was a slight delay. This is Russia, the entrepreneur figured, and such delays are commonplace. He had no choice but to wait. Soon he discovered the real reason for the stall: The printer had printed the first batch for himself and was selling thousands of copies outside of Moscow.

Piracy of software, books, videotapes and music cassettes is a widespread and accepted practice in Russia. These items are sold openly in shops without fear of confiscation. Although Russia is a signatory to the Berne Convention on intellectual property rights, the enforcement of antipiracy laws will take some time.

Most Russians have no uneasiness about violating intellectual property laws, as the idea of private property is fairly new. In addition, acquiring and copying is a culturally rooted practice in Russia. Nearly every time Russia made a surge forward in development, for example, in building St. Petersburg, Western technology and expertise were brought in for guidance. In many instances, Western ways were simply copied. The famous Soviet T-34 tank of the World War II era, for instance, hailed as an evolutionary breakthrough, copies its suspension system from an American designer and its engine from the Italians.

In 1919, Soviet Russia, adhering to Marx, determined that original inventions were the property of the state. The inventor's name was registered with the product and if it proved successful, he received a small reward. That remained unchanged until 1992, when two new laws were formed: the patent law of the Russian federation and the law on trademarks, service marks and the names of the places of origin of goods (factory names, for example). But, they fall short of protecting against theft of intellectual property.

No comprehensive intellectual property law to protect both foreign and Russian products has been formed. In fact, the government is beginning to fear for the theft of its own technology. There is no real right to ownership of scientific achievements and export of technologies. Certain ministries, such as the Ministry of Nuclear Power, do strictly control their technology, but other industries trade technologies virtually without control. A Russian firm typically concludes a contract with a foreign firm without specific clauses detailing intellectual property rights, potentially resulting in the government's loss of billions of dollars.

Information

While smoking a cigarette, an employee enters data from a massive stack of papers into a computer. She works in the St. Petersburg government office responsible for registering foreign joint ventures. It's the second time the office is attempting to computerize their information. Before, the antiquated 286 computer crashed, and all was lost.

The agency struggles with handling all statistics. They cannot say how many joint ventures are from Finland, for example, because the information isn't organized in such a way. Nor can they determine how much foreign money has been invested in the city: When the partners of the joint ventures initially registered the amount of capitalization, untrained staff added the rouble amount and dollar amount together—without first converting them to the same currency.

Russia has never held information in high esteem for both political and technological reasons, except for small sectors in the government, which excelled at gathering and documenting intelligence for the state. Now that foreign business and ideas are flooding in, the country is unequipped to handle the resulting information surge. The poor information culture goes hand in hand with a general business culture already disinclined to spend time analyzing information for the most effective decision making.

Information is often poorly collected or not gathered at all. It is inefficiently organized and often not released, either for reasons of lingering secrecy, lack of computers and methods to process it or because of the prevailing belief that the public simply has no need to know. Complicating the problem is the Russian person's reluctance to give out information. A tradition of secrecy stemming from past times still influences people's attitudes. When it comes to financial information, Russians also tend to keep quiet for fear of attracting organized crime.

Even the simplest information may need to be hunted down and verified. Just keeping up with the outside world is still difficult in most cities. Foreign newspapers arrive late and only in Moscow and St. Petersburg; magazines are limited, and on-line computer databases are often hindered by poor telephone lines.

The foreign visitor should also know that sometimes what appears to be legitimate information in the Russian media may not be factual. Newspaper articles typically offer news without attribution and allegations are made without foundation. Twisting facts to conform to an idea was an impressive Soviet skill. Today, journalists are paid handsomely to devise an article that appears to be objective but in reality has its content dictated by the person commissioning it. Such articles are called *skritaya reklama* or "hidden advertising" and journalists often solicit politicians and businesspeople for the lucrative articles.

Many people also question the accuracy of government statistics, which have traditionally been doctored to please Communist Party officials. Moreover, finding the exact department and person who holds the required information could take weeks. Arcane, sinister Russian bureaucracies have been written about by Gogol and Dostoyevsky.

However, responding to the need for reliable information, private marketing research companies and information consultancies have set up in some large Russian cities.

Company Information

Standard company information such as annual reports, public relations brochures and product data is scarcely available. Managers may not know their own company's internal situation. They have little more than production figures to guide them. It can be guesswork judging the size of a potential market, or even finding the most cost-effective contractor to supply materials for a project.

Russian companies do compile statistics, but they don't know how to handle them in terms of profit, according to Alexander Sapozhnikov, CIS director of Image Alpha Ltd., a Moscow-based consultancy. Sapozhnikov recalls a factory which boasted it made $15 million. But when his consultancy examined the books, calculating wages and expenses, they found that the factory barely broke even. "Large Russian companies don't understand the correlation between revenues and expenses," Sapozhnikov explains.

Another example concerns a Moscow factory which received an order for the production of ladies' wool coats from an Asian firm. The Russian director promised an $8 per unit price tag and the deal was ready to be inked, but at the negotiation stage, when labor and overhead were added in, the director's cost jumped to $16 per unit. The foreign side was confused: electricity and labor were comparatively cheaper than in the West, so why did the cost per unit jump? The director explained that his big factory must maintain an employee vacation house, a children's camp and medical facilities. These facilities were installed during Soviet times and employees have grown used to them.

Information Safety

The now-defunct KGB used incredibly sophisticated surveillance methods to investigate, monitor and harass anybody they wanted to. Information on every citizen was meticulously documented. They tapped telephones, bugged flats and hotels, monitored foreigners' movements, cracked computer passwords. The KGB is gone, in its place is the Federal Counter-Intelligence Service, but the data, expertise and information-collecting tools remain. Some ex-KGB agents now devote their time to economic espionage.

Moreover, Russia is full of brilliant engineers who can make a computer from scratch, create or debug complex software viruses, or repair a fax machine without glancing at a wiring schematic. These technicians are often poorly paid state enterprise employees who secretly use their skills in some entrepreneurial effort. It's reasonable to assume they are hired to tamper with telephones and computers.

It's advisable for the foreign businessperson to be overconcerned about finding and plugging information leaks. Precious information from accountancy firms, the tax department, customs, police and various municipal offices is officially confidential. But during Russia's drifting transition to a free market system, nothing can be guaranteed. Press reports claim such agencies collaborate with specific business interests or criminal groups to provide information. Moreover, foreigners who don't fully grasp the situation in the city unknowingly leak the information themselves.

Information leaks often come from colleagues at work. Local employees can be easily recruited with cash since they earn so little. Few people, preferably one or two, should have access to financial information, and few colleagues should know the manager's home phone or address.

There are secure banks, but it's best to choose one on recommendations from another foreign company. In any business transaction, when company *A* transfers money to company *B*, all the details of the transaction go into a database at the bank. Through careless security, bribes or threats, information can be leaked. But the information on big money transactions, sources say, comes from partners and colleagues who are in the know.

All financial information, even the most seemingly innocuous, is better kept private. Russians like to ask a foreigner how much he earns or if he owns a house in his home country. Simple curiosity is at work, but information can be inadvertently leaked. In Russian business, a good practice is to get into the habit of answering all personal questions in broad, general terms: for example, "Where do you live?" "In the south of the city;" "Where is Mr. Smith?" "He's busy." Russians often communicate this way, without detail. Openness was dangerous for decades—until the mid-1980s.

Advertising: Brand Names

Halikan is a notebook computer which made its debut in Eastern Europe and is selling briskly in Russia. Many Russians perceive the product to be at the same level as IBM or Hewlett Packard, but outside of Russia and Eastern Europe, Halikan remains relatively unknown, merely one of the many notebook PCs made in Taiwan. The Halikan notebook is made by Taiwan-based Chaplet Systems and through the advertising efforts of Chaplet's Russian distributor, the product's brand name recognition blossomed.

Russia is a great leveling field. Company names, trademarks and slogans so obviously familiar to the Western consumer have less recognition in Russia. The possibilities for building a brand name product from scratch and raising it to the level of a famous multinational product are strong. Similarly, a multinational can introduce new products into the undersupplied Russian market and score big—as electronics giant Texas Instruments (TI) did by becoming one of the leaders in laser printer sales in the Czech market. (TI does not sell laser printers outside of the Czech Republic.)

Building a brand name, however, requires substantial investment in advertising. Russia spans eleven time zones and covers roughly one tenth of the world. Newspapers, with mainly local circulations, offer limited coverage. Moreover, once an ad is placed it's difficult to check publication distribution points across such a huge country. A company cannot be certain its ad campaign reaches all the cities promised.

To create brand awareness, television has been the most effective answer. Television is an incredibly powerful medium in Russia. Broadcasts can extend to the country's far reaches and simply by tuning in, company officials can ensure their ads have been on the air. Also, in the past everything broadcast was government sanctioned. Many people, especially older generations, find it hard to imagine a lie on television. As for popularity, a Russian may not have a car or washing machine, but nearly every family has a television.

Products such as Snickers, Tampax and Uncle Ben's food products are recognized by a vast majority of the country mainly because of television ad campaigns. Advertising, especially "saturation" campaigns, has fueled some resentment. Until the late 1980s, there was virtually no product advertising in all of Russia. Suddenly an ad blitz from the West, bursting with color and gimmickry, floods television and radio, appears in newspapers and on billboards. Even the subway systems in Moscow and St. Petersburg, whose architects prided themselves on aesthetically pure station construction, now display ad placards.

After an initial fascination, some people express anger and resentment at the cheapness and superficiality of advertising. Foreign companies, with free-flowing money and ideas, have bought the majority of airtime. Russian products are rarely advertised, often for lack of money to pay rising advertising costs. Some say this sends a message that Russian products and services are inferior to foreign ones.

To some, foreign product ads are seen as an intrusion and negative influence in Russia. Sociologists complain that children today can name the foreign candy bars but cannot recite the poetry of Alexander Pushkin, as they could in the past.

Finding the Right Approach

Advertising reveals the magic that a culture believes in. But what is effective in one country can sometimes be confusing in another. In fact, Russians sometimes cannot understand what foreign advertisers are trying to sell in their campaigns.

Max Troshichev, writing in the *St. Petersburg Press* English-language newspaper, tells a story about the early advertising efforts of U.S. manufacturer Proctor & Gamble from a Russian perspective. In 1991, the company began promoting *Vidal Sassoon Wash-and-Go Shampoo-and- Conditioner-in-One* in Russia. At first, success was overwhelming, but management didn't realize the real reason for the success: It was the only Western quality shampoo in Russia at the time. The shampoo ads

> were uninformative—they didn't try to explain what "conditioner" was to a population used to bland, unso-phisticated products. In the Russian language, *conditioner* means air conditioner and nothing else. The rest of the product name is even more interesting. *Vidal* means I saw or Did you see? depending on intonation. *Sassoon* sounds like *sosun* politely translated as *sucking*. *Wash* sounds like *vosh* (there is no W in Russian) which means louse. And now try to imagine what the whole package *Vidal Sassoon Wash-and-Go* means to uninformed Russians, plus the mysterious *Shampoo-and-Conditioner-in-One*. The company ignored the misunderstandings. Competition came in and now their shampoo sells only moderately well in Russia. Ad money was wasted and they missed a market they had a good chance to conquer.

Many companies have made mistakes, according to Troshichev. A Camel cigarettes television ad shows a stylishly rugged man paddling in wild rivers or driving a Jeep through thick jungle. There is a somewhat rude expression in Russian: *eskyat na zhopu prekluchenny* ("to look for adventures on one's ass") meaning courting trouble by doing something useless and dangerously stupid. "The Russian is reminded of this expression when watching the Camel man's adventurous deeds," Troshichev writes.

> The ads depict Camel as a symbol of fun and adventure. But parachuting, canoeing and jeep riding are so terribly removed from the Russian way of life that viewers see only a fool risking his neck for nothing. Nearly the same can be said about other cigarette ads. They show lifestyles absolutely alien to Russia and fail to create much response besides bewilderment. American cigarettes are popular, but most people say it makes no difference whether they smoke Camel, Marlboro or another brand.

A foreign company should seriously consider hiring a Russian advertising manager and public relations representative. Foreign companies should be cautious using ad campaigns created for the Western market because the response in Russia will be unpredictable. UK-based Cadbury was wise enough to introduce its *Spiral* chocolate bar in Russia as *Spira*. Read by a Russian, *Spiral* would become *speeral*, the word for intrauterine device.

Who's That Guy?

Words aren't the only area of confusion. Widely-recognized Western icons fail to register in the Russian mind. For example, a foreign design studio in St. Petersburg preparing an advertisement for an American film festival to be pitched at Russians began by putting Humphrey Bogart on the promotional material. Every Russian in the office who saw the ad asked, "Who's that guy?" Russians also react differently to colors. Swedish automaker Volvo did research which found Russians prefer cars in green or red—colors positively unpopular in the U.S. market.

American Hillary Greene, who spent three years in Russia at a Swedish advertising firm, says Western companies can best position themselves in the Russian market by starting from the beginning, by assuming the product is new and the consumer knows nothing. For example, one company that got it right was U.S.-based Tambrands, manufacturer of Tampax, which entered a market where millions of women were unfamiliar with factory-made tampons. A Western ad campaign would fall flat: Western tampon ads normally show women actively taking part in sports or leisure, only alluding to the product. So in Russia, Tambrands promoted its product through educational advertisements and programs in schools, using Russian health experts with diagrams to explain how the product is used.

Tambrands is the exception. The typical head office just wants the Western advertisement translated. Many TV ads are Western imports with Russian voice-overs.

The Ad Hit Squad

The Russian government imposes some strict and perhaps unusual restrictions on advertising. To retain the purity of the Russian language, an advertising task force operates in Moscow and St. Petersburg to enforce local ad laws. For example, business names using variations of the word *Russia* will bring a heavy fine: The government has declared the name *Russia* must be used in a respectful way. Advertisements also must include a Russian language translation; in print ads the Cyrillic translation must be of equal size to the foreign language (brand names are exempt).

In St. Petersburg, an advertising *hit-squad* roams the city and dismantles outdoor advertising without a Cyrillic translation. Moreover, certain symbols may only be used on logos and advertising after the payment of a fee. Moscow has its own peculiarities. A city decree demands that all shops on the main streets have attractive window displays. Therefore, the foreign company should consult locals about advertising laws.

Sales: A New Concept

Because of poor distribution and an undersupplied market, Russia remains a seller's paradise, not a consumer market. Russia has no long-standing traditions of selling. The prosperous traders of Russia's past were generally foreigners or a small percentage of people from nobility, approved by the ruling elite. During Soviet times, trading was conducted at a ministry level, so market savvy never really had a chance to develop within Russian culture. In fact until 1991, buying from one place and selling in another was considered "speculation," a crime punishable by a mandatory two-year imprisonment.

Prior to 1991, profit per units sold wasn't important and there were no sales commissions. If a product was bad, there was no reason to keep it secret because plenty of replacements, churned out by the massive state factories, were readily available. Even today the relationship between salesclerk and customer involves blind trust. Customers will ask Russian store clerks if the bread is fresh, if the model of toaster is good, or if the cheese is delicious. The clerk will likely answer truthfully, without hesitation. This lack of shifty salespersons is refreshing, although with the appearance of the profit motive this promises to quickly change.

It should be no surprise that basic sales techniques have proved surprisingly effective in Russia. For example, a foreign clothing salesman ended his presentation to Russian buyers by giving the prospective buyer several options—but not including the option to refuse altogether: "Do you want 100 cartons in red, 50 cartons in red and 50 cartons in blue, or 100 cartons in assorted colors?" He has had a string of successes using such elementary techniques.

Unsophisticated consumers and lack of regulation have rewarded ambitious hucksters. Similar to the untamed West in nineteenth-century America, Russia has salesmen with flashy appeal and questionable techniques trying to make a fast buck with crudely obvious scams such as bait and switch and pyramid investment funds.

Selling and Marketing

Soviet companies focused strictly on government-specified production. Sales and marketing didn't exist because they weren't necessary. A company produced a product and consistently delivered pre-established quantities to a centralized distributor, who would in turn dole them out to the proper stores around the USSR. The factory manufacturing bicycles, for example, was freed from concerns after delivering a large quantity of acceptable bikes to a distributor. It essentially "turned in" the product and went back to producing.

Today, the absence of sales and marketing experience cripples many Russian companies trying to sell their products or concepts in competitive markets. Russians are only now discovering how necessary it is to think of a product in terms of sophistication, design, uniqueness and quality and to offer follow-up service.

Market research firms, both foreign and Russian, have set up in Moscow and St. Petersburg. Yet typically, Russian companies do insufficient market research before launching their product or service. Since most of the Russian market is underserviced and undersupplied in almost every area, this problem hasn't become apparent. Giving to the market rather than inquiring what the market needs is the fundamental attitude.

Foreigners who do business with Russian companies say factory directors and managers typically don't know how much to charge for their products. They rarely know their production costs and find it difficult to tell a buyer what to pay. Managers still don't comprehend the idea of product quality.

According to Robert Farish, an electronics analyst in Moscow, if, for example, a component needs to be slotted onto a circuit board, the dimensions must be exact. The pins cannot be slightly long and a square part cannot be a little uneven—or the fit may not be exact. Yet factory managers still adopt the attitude that if a part was good enough for a mighty MIG-23 fighter jet, it should be good enough for a little personal computer.

For foreign companies in Russia, moving the product is not difficult. The hard part is getting those involved in the sales and marketing process to understand the basic concepts behind sales. Purchasing managers at stores must be convinced to merchandise a product, display it properly, sell it at the correct price and request more when stock is exhausted. Foreign companies spend long hours educating salespeople as well as buyers and store clerks in these concepts.

A foreign sales manager who was brought in to manage a new sales department for a U.S. company manufacturing in Russia says he spent nearly all his time in the field.

I realized when I came here that people didn't know about selling, so I had to call up all my training and experience from Western markets. It was necessary to convince the salespeople, at every step, that what they are doing is correct. Because you educate people in sales and they come back and say "No, this is not the way you do it, you have to do it this way." In their mind they have been thinking that way all the time. Only training, going out into the field, showing them, that's how you overcome it. There have been negative opinions from salespeople we were training and we try to work that into positive opinions. It takes a lot of close attention, patience and respect to the people. Often a new idea or approach must be repeated hundreds of times before it goes into the mind of a person in Russia. And at the same time we are educating the sales team, we educate the buyer and consumer and counter salesgirl.

Some foreign businesspeople will insist that in Russia, distribution is everything. Reliable distribution channels are only beginning to form. Large distributors cannot possibly cover the expanse of Russia. If a company really wants distribution for a product, says one foreign businessperson, people must go from door to door selling it. Foreign companies which fail at distribution have made the mistake of following the same approach in Russia as they do in the West, he adds, "When you go on those lines, you may not fail, but you are asking too much from the locals, and they aren't capable of providing it."

U.K.-based Tambrands, which manufactures Tampax in Russia, tried to expand its distribution outlets by getting Tampax into department stores and food stores. Company officials initially met with resistance to the idea. Department store managers insisted that Tampax was only to be sold in pharmacies, and food store purchasing managers explained that their stores sell only food. Tambrands' strategy was a slow, modest approach, convincing the buyers to try only a few cartons of Tampax, even though higher volumes could be sold. When the product sold out, the company was able to slowly increase the volume, but only after much resistance. The department store manager insisted that the product was selling well in the location, display and quantity that was decided on initially, and was puzzled and irritated when the Tambrands sales manager wanted to modify the sales strategy. Since product sales were going well, he reasoned, why would anybody want to change things? Tambrands' polite persistence eventually solved the problem and the product is now enormously successful in Russia.

Sales Outlets

Several levels of sales outlets prevail. The most basic level involves someone standing near a subway station holding, for example, a pair of shoes. Pensioners often stand in line at state shops to buy food products and resell them at a higher price at night when the shops are closed. At markets and transportation terminals throughout big cities, lines of people holding single items are a typical sight.

The next step up is a person with a table on the street who carts his goods to and from the site every day. Young couples often sell fruit or ice cream this way to make a living. Then comes the abundant kiosk—a thin, often dilapidated metal shed that sits in every city and village in Russia. Kiosks sell small quantities of inconsistently supplied goods, often at higher prices than the shop. Kiosks are presumably the precursor to the convenience store. Fruit and vegetables, newspapers, clothes, electronic goods and hamburgers are some of the items sold from kiosks. Most foreign companies, however, refuse to distribute through kiosks because local governments are trying to abolish the majority of them.

On a higher level are the small shops, often with a staff smaller than five. Many are privately run. Larger state-run stores include the *Dieta*, *Universam*, and *Univermag*. Each has strictly defined product lines. A food store carries only basic food items, a pharmacy handles only pharmaceuticals, and a *parfumerie*, only perfumes. A department store (*Univermag*) differs significantly from a shiny, well-stocked Western department store. It does include product departments such as sporting goods, men's and women's clothing and furniture, but widespread product shortages and bankrupt factories have limited the variety available.

Moreover, infrastructure, lighting, displays, cash registers, floors and walls are drab and outmoded. Russian department stores characteristically employ excess staff and do everything themselves—storage, warehousing, maintenance, security, display, and sales.

At the wholesale level, Russian companies often work without salespeople, advertising large quantities of goods in newspapers. Another method is for manufacturers or wholesalers to employ a *torgovyoi agyent* or trade agent. Similar to commission agents, they represent many companies at once. A trade agent may have a list of a hundred various products and visit several store purchasing agents each day. Chances are the shop buyers will want one or two of the items on the list, and the agent gets a percentage of each order.

Managing the Steady Drop

In the past, Soviet citizens stood in line for food. Today, a line most likely means Russian citizens, roused by a rumor or feeling of a steep rouble rate decline, are quickly buying dollars at the lowest rate possible as an inflation hedge.

As of January 1, 1994, a presidential decree ordered all cash transactions to be conducted in roubles only. (Credit card purchases and some bank transfers may be in hard currency.) Since then, any big drop or anticipated big drop in the value of the rouble to the dollar prompts businesspeople to take special precautions. Retailers, who receive a constant inflow of roubles, may send employees to the bank every three hours with a sack of roubles. If rumors that the exchange rate will drop steeply suddenly prove true, the company wants as many roubles as possible converted into more stable U.S. dollars to preserve profit.

Roubles, though, seem to be a front for an underlying dollar-based economy. Foreign manufacturers, joint venture restaurants and companies selling imported goods invariably ask for the rouble equivalent of the listed dollar price. Invoices may carry the conversion rate to be used. It is often expressed as the Central Bank of Russia (CBR) rate on the day of payment.

Similarly, all companies must pay their employees a rouble salary. To better provide a stable wage, foreign companies pay the rouble equivalent of a dollar amount—which Russians see as an attractive aspect of working for a foreign company. Wages of most Russian workers are not adjusted for inflation and some employers delay payroll to reduce the cost of paying salaries.

State-run companies and services tend not to use a dollar benchmark and as a result suffer losses. A twenty-million-rouble telephone bill begins to look much less daunting to a company which knows it can hold the bill and watch the rouble's daily slide. The telephone company, without computers and efficient management, is unequipped to stop the losses.

Companies sometimes gain advantage by acting quickly during a sudden drop in the rouble's value. If the rouble drops steeply in one day, money pours into firms from debtor clients they may not even remember. At the same time, each firm receiving the roubles tries to pay them out to someone else as fast as possible before they devalue further.

With so much money flying around so rapidly, a temporary business paralysis can set in. Until the rouble settles again, many companies will not accept new orders paid for by bank transfer, even though bank transfers are required for the conduct of all legal business. One answer is that firms will bill with today's prices, but insist on an extra premium to allow for inflation before the money transfer can be effected. In times of rapid movement those premiums have been up to twenty percent.

The rouble appears to have achieved relative stability in 1995, but that could change. For most companies in Russia, a steadily dropping rouble is treated as an inevitable fact of life. They try to minimize losses, but accept them as normal.

Tax Inspection

A businessperson in Russia wanted to set up a credit card payment system abroad to attract foreign customers. Aware of the swift and sure punishments for illegal offshore transactions, an inquiry was sent to the Central Bank of Russia, asking whether it was legal for credit card payments to go to a foreign bank. Months later, a three-paragraph letter arrived which explained that such a situation was not yet covered by Russian law. The hapless firm didn't know how to proceed. There was no indication of whether such a law was in the works or if companies were allowed to establish the payment mechanism. Although no law stated it was illegal, the businessperson decided against it because of a tendency to backdate incoming legislation and fine "lawbreakers."

Russia's notorious taxation system has been the most obstructing mechanism for foreign businesses. Arcane and fickle, severe and unfair, the tax system works against long-term investment and the development of a growth strategy. Monitoring and interpreting Russia's tax system requires extreme vigilance.

A Coopers & Lybrand tax manager writing in the *American Chamber of Commerce in Russia* journal put it this way: "Russian tax law is unmodified, evolving rapidly and is often imprecise." A company operating in Moscow, for example, may be liable to pay more than twenty different taxes. Employer payroll tax contributions are a prime example as they include tax contributions to four different social funds. These are police tax; pension fund tax; road tax and medical insurance tax. To cut down on tax cheats, Russia has established a no-nonsense tax inspection agency (*nalog inspektsia*).

In the past, the mere suggestion of a KGB visit terrified a person. Today, the tax inspection officer seems to have a similar awesome reputation. Tax inspectors can arrive unannounced and should they uncover errors or manipulations, penalties may be three or more times the amount of the indiscretion. Conventional persuasion—bribes or the use of connections—has limited appeal: the inspectors receive a healthy percentage of the fine imposed.

The tax penalty system is severe. In particular, there is no distinction between innocent error and deliberate mistake. Yet mistakes are common because legislation is complex and unclear. Tax inspectors are often unfamiliar with what are normal commercial transactions in the West, so there is a tendency to assume that anything that is unfamiliar to them is tax fraud.

Get a Real Accountant

A small company in the U.S. enlists the part-time help of an accountant who maybe checks the books once a week. In Russia, the same small company would need to employ a full-time accountant and assistant. Larger companies will have legions of them. They will probably be the busiest people on the staff because Russia's requirements for tax and financial information are complex, inefficient, draconian and fickle, and accounting requires a labor-intensive approach.

Soviet-era prices did not change for decades at a time, but in the post-communist era they move weekly, if not daily. Inflation continually renders meaningless rouble limits set on various aspects of spending and many accountants are struggling to keep up in this dynamic environment.

Yet the title "accountant" is dangerously misleading. In communist Russia, there were no accountants. Like so many other oddities in the Russian business culture, this one is something an outsider cannot fathom until the consequences become dramatically apparent. And yet it is easily explained.

The Russian word for accountant, *bookhalter*, comes straight from the German *buchhalter*—which means bookkeeper. And keeping books is exactly what the Russian accountant does. The Soviet enterprise had no equivalent to the Western accountant.

Under the command economy there was no need for the average enterprise to make forecasts about the future. Everything was planned. The financial future was dictated by a central authority rather than a fluctuating market—Russia's famed five-year plans were the most obvious sign of that central planning. Costs were fixed and as a result prices were stable. (Russians are fond of remembering that public transport prices remained exactly the same for forty years after World War II.)

The *bookhalter* was trained to work in an environment in which many of the factors he dealt with (raw material costs, wages, taxes, etc.) were so static that simply counting them, rather than analyzing them, was enough. Because profit and loss were not vital signs of financial health, there was no need to rigorously monitor the balance sheet. The *bookhalter* merely recorded production information as opposed to analyzing financial data, a practice which remains today.

So it should be no surprise Russian accountants excel at bookkeeping. The Soviet bureaucracy expected enormous detail. *Bookhalters* will be able to determine what has happened to the smallest component of a tractor at a huge plant. But ask how much profit the company will make over the next six months and they are lost. Profit forecasting is a mystery, as is cash flow planning as opposed to cash flow watching.

Therefore, a foreign businessperson is well advised to remember that the *bookhalter* records transactions, pays bills and generally watches the cash flow. He does not forecast, budget or plan for taxes like his Western counterpart. And he is more likely to detail the amount of tax payments rather than suggesting strategies for reducing the tax burden.

The bulk of Russian accountants remain the old traditional type. Traditional Soviet accountants often lead their firms into marginal or unprofitable positions. They tend to collect information for the sake of collecting it in hopes of pleasing the chief executive and the tax bureaucracy. Moreover, as information collectors rather than analysts, they often do not understand how to present figures in a way that is useful to managers.

One foreign joint-venture partner was stunned when his chief *bookhalter* casually informed him that a huge taxation payment was due in ten days. (The figure was equal to two weeks gross earnings for the firm.) There had been no attempt to spread the tax payment over several quarters, thereby reducing the burden. The accountant was not being obstructive; she had simply not thought to include it in the quarterly plan, which she clearly did not understand or value.

Not only does the *bookhalter* lack the experience to value financial predictions, there is a tendency among Russians to undervalue the benefits of doing so. Many Russian firms lurch from one cash crisis to the next. One Russian company director, the head of a travel agency specializing in sending Russians abroad—a highly competitive business—visited the office of his friend, a foreign manager. The foreigner was examining a simple budget for the coming quarter. The Russian director was fascinated. He asked for an explanation and commented that a budget was a good idea and he might try something similar at his firm. His turnover is about $1 million a year.

But today a new breed of accountants are emerging. They have spent time in the West or worked with Western accounting firms in Russia. New companies are snapping up these trained accountants, while some of the promising older enterprises push their accountants to provide financial planning.

Finally, foreign companies in Russia should not work solely with a Russian *bookhalter*. A consultant at a foreign accounting firm (which generally retains both foreign and Russian accountants) can be enlisted for guidance. At the very least, the experts say, hire a traditional Russian *bookhalter* to do number crunching, but employ as a supervisor at least one "New Russian" *bookhalter* who understands Western practices.

Organized Crime

Try to find the office of a normally high-profile Western company in Russia. Often it's unmarked or hidden away inside a modest building. It's no secret that organized crime is widespread and influential in Russia. Contact with criminal elements is a part of doing business and unfortunately, opinions from all quarters agree that will remain a reality for some time.

Organized crime has flourished since the collapse of the Soviet Union in 1991 and the target of the Mafia-like groups is business—Russian and foreign. Shootouts in the streets are unlikely. But business communities in virtually all Russian cities share a silent understanding that extortion is widespread and government research supports that notion.

Russia's racketeers are not just one or two monolithic groups, but various smaller, nimble organizations that have emerged to get a foot in the extortion market. Each group varies in the level of sophistication. At the low end are loosely organized street thugs who persuade their victims by threats of physical violence. At the top end are more complex, well-connected organizations that prefer refined tactics. Such criminal groups have proven to have tentacles in the government, the military, the police force, the customs department, the tax department and banks.

Criminal groups thrive partly because law enforcement agencies are impoverished. Police, who earn the equivalent of $100 per month and drive rickety cars, don't have the equipment or will, to effectively combat criminals who cruise around in imported luxury cars and can buy sophisticated weapons.

Criminals especially covet foreign businesses, which they believe are respectable in the eyes of the government and handsomely prosperous. Racketeers may demand payments for protection of the business and employees. Other groups may need to launder money. Laws covering the settling of business debts are only evolving and an unprotected business can easily be cheated without recourse. Business partners, accountants, banks and a company security team must be chosen with extreme care in Russia.

Problems with organized crime can be compared to the risk of illness from a tropical disease when on vacation. Neither should dissuade the pioneer from taking the journey—and both require precautions. But before doing business in Russia, consult foreign businesspersons who are already doing business there. Russia's market beckons, but naiveté will be punished.

Personal Security

Russia is in the midst of dramatic fundamental change. Old systems are collapsing, and new systems are struggling to form. Social systems such as education, law and law enforcement, transport and health care are in a severe crisis. Wealth is being redistributed. The crime rate is soaring. Such conditions prevent Russian cities from comparison to U.S. or European cities. Life is wildly unpredictable, even though surface appearance is one of apparent stability. Foreign businesspersons should expect their stay in Russia to be adventurous.

In Russia, all foreigners are presumed to be rich and are often targeted for crime. The new foreign visitor should take precautions he would take in any large U.S. city—and in addition, be guided by a trusted Russian contact and keep a low profile.

7
FOREIGN MANAGERS IN RUSSIA

Culture Shock

Foreign visitors who have never visited the former Eastern Bloc countries will feel varying degrees of culture shock when they visit Russia. Russia always has been, and still is, something in between European and Asian cultures.

Culture shock manifests itself in various ways and can strike with differing degrees. It can build up slowly over time or hit hard, all at once.

Not being able to read or speak Russian can send foreigners into serious culture shock, especially those who feel comfortable only when they are in control. Not knowing Russian keeps them on the periphery of the culture and floundering in ambiguity.

For an educated person used to relying on his communicative skills, frustration can quickly set in when he is unfamiliar with the language. Foreigners can become virtually helpless without their interpreters. They become dependent on them not just for everyday communication but for simple tasks such as finding restaurants and hailing a taxi. Without these language skills cultural contact is curtailed.

Although learning the Russian language might be beyond the commitment that some businesspeople want to make, even a familiarity with a phrase book could break barriers and lessen culture shock. Learning to read the Cyrillic alphabet is not very complicated or time consuming and being able to read the words is rewarding.

In Russia, culture shock commonly produces one of two reactions. Foreigners become contemptuous of Russia and its people, finding fault in almost all situations, or they may become uncritically accepting, even submissive, in the face of the Russians they meet. The first reaction would make a bad impression anywhere in the world. While foreigners who lean too far the other way, suspending their critical faculties, leave themselves open to exploitation.

There is also the tendency for foreigners with little international experience to interpret Russian attitudes and behavior using their own cultural terms. A Caucasian businessperson facing a Japanese, Korean or Indian counterpart most likely sees that he is dealing with a foreign culture with different customs and mores. But Russian people resemble Americans or Europeans and it is tempting for visitors from those regions to assume they are the same when they aren't. Visitors making this mistake often react emotionally, insisting the Russian way is irrational and wrong.

Culture shock comes not only from attitudes, but also from living conditions. The phrase *Third World* implies the existence of a First and Second World. Russia falls neatly into the Second World category, sandwiched between the developing countries and post-industrial, information-based ones.

Na Remont (Under Repair)

Na remont (under repair or renovation) is likely to be one of the first Russian phrases a foreigner learns. Anything can be *na remont* at any time, without warning, for any length of time. Sites *na remont* are treated with a great deal of cynicism by Russian people. A road will be completely ripped up, rendering it unusable, and earth-moving equipment sits idle on the site for months. "*Na remont*," a Russian will explain, and nothing further needs to be said.

Time for repairs to be completed can be considerable. A successful shop owner who decides to remodel or expand the premises may need to close down the business for three months in order for the job to be completed. Usually the shop owner will not try to question the repair team's estimated completion time since repairmen are considered experts and their word cannot be debated.

On the individual level, a *remontnik* (repairperson) is perhaps a friend of a friend who comes to the home to fix a water heater, install a door lock or hang a new lamp. A *remontnik* may have *zoloteya ruki* (golden hands), which means he or she can repair that which others have declared unrepairable. The *remontnik* may not own a wide range of equipment and the job may be a *somopol*, meaning a makeshift job or rigging a solution from materials at hand.

Arrogance

When the pre-Revolutionary plumbing system causes water to drip onto the computers, or the company car has been at the mechanic for two weeks and employees habitually arrive ten minutes late, smiling, it's tempting to yell something like, "Doesn't anything in this %$*!#$! country work right?"

Foreign visitors working in Russia should bring deep reserves of patience. The best policy is to resist the temptation to identify and ridicule Russia's shortcomings in front of Russians. Russians know the infrastructure is dated and causes repeated inconveniences. When foreigners point it out, Russians will be deeply offended without showing it.

Foreigners should be especially patient when dealing with people. Russian managers tell stories of the arrogance of some foreign businesspeople. Foreigners have a tendency to believe that if a Russian is paid $150 a month his abilities justify that wage. A Western manager who studied at Harvard tends to base his judgment on the premise that his Russian counterpart who studied in Petrozavodsk is inferior. Yet in reality, plenty of Russians hold expertise comparable to or better than their Western counterparts.

It is a common mistake for foreigners to observe that Russians look European, and to therefore assume that Russians must be thinking in a reasonable European way. When they don't, arrogance may flare. The fact that Russians are not from a cultural background similar to Western Europeans does not make them inferior.

Criticizing the Past

Trying to score points off of any Russian by trashing the former Soviet system can seriously backfire. An Australian described how he mockingly referred to the "radiant future" (*svetloye budushcheye*—a standard piece of Communist Party rhetoric, which the population strived toward) in conversation with a Russian industrial tycoon, only to be explicitly told that the earlier generation genuinely believed in that concept, and that this was not a bad thing.

Nor is it wise to refer disparagingly to concepts or institutions which the person sitting across the desk from you may have invested his life in, only to see dreams crumble as the old order faded. Russians feel that individuals who did not have to make the choices that they were forced to make should not criticize the former system.

Certainly some Russians feel nostalgic when looking back to a time of crime-free, cheap living under the Communists, which contrasts sharply with the grim present. It is common to hear that life was better under Brezhnev, while some older people remember the Stalinist era with affection.

Dealing With Head Office: "What's Going On Out There?"

The distant head office can develop into an adversary, questioning situations that undoubtedly seem way outside the logic of even the senior businessperson's experience. Foreign managers in Russia report that bosses outside the country fail to realize the difficulty of completing simple tasks, such as getting an employee's visa in order.

Just think of the possible reactions of Chicago, London or Frankfurt if they are told the goods they sent vanished from the customs warehouse yet the bill for storage must still be paid; that fiscal year figures will take weeks rather than days to calculate; or that a scheduled factory construction has stopped because an entire region has run out of two-meter, concrete-reinforcing steel rods.

The foreign manager should assure his superiors that unorthodox methods will be required in a country that demands unusual flexibility. For example, Russian operations run better in a vertically integrated company structure, a concept that Western industry has left well behind. McDonald's now grows its own vegetables outside of Moscow to ensure quality supplies to its operations. Likewise, a Swedish-run hotel had to open its own management and training school in Russia to ensure qualified staff would be available in the future.

Company financial matters can cause the most friction between the Russian office and headquarters. Finding $3.5 million in unreceipted, unaudited hard currency earnings in the company safe, as one American accountant did, would unnerve even the most understanding home office. Compounding these frustrations is a faulty communication system. The home office calls, but can't get through; they send a fax but on the receiving end the message is illegible, or they want information in a few hours, but it takes days and is only partially complete.

Reporting on problems as well as successes could save problems later. More important, though, head office officials should be strongly encouraged to visit their Russian operation to understand the framework within which employees must work.

8
RUSSIAN WORK ATTITUDES

The New Russians

In Russia, a small percentage of the population has grown extremely wealthy. Many of the *Novie Russkie* (New Russians) as they are often called, have made millions of dollars in less than a year. New Russians are not simply rich businesspeople in the traditional sense. Few have recognized professions, almost all are men and there is not even a loose link between their education and wealth.

The New Russians are *beeznismyeni*, a term often used in a derogatory sense as a synonym for borderline criminal. Such a businessperson is often a high-rolling entrepreneur with little patience for a balance sheet or earnings forecast. The New Russian wants to do a deal now, with little research and scant paperwork. He does things his way, through connections and manipulation, and knows only victory—and great victory at that. Currency speculation, sales of raw materials abroad, real estate sales, pyramid investment scams, tax-free buying and selling of goods, and organized criminal activities are some of the ways high earnings have been possible.

New Russians and their families vigorously acquire everything that is imported, and then show it off. While the Mercedes Benz has become the prize symbol of this wealth, the gold watch, cellular telephone, imported silk suit and Italian shoes comprise the uniform. New Russians dine in expensive restaurants as a practice and plunk down fortunes at casinos.

This small percentage of wealthy Russians likely have associations with organized criminal groups. Others made their first money trading on the streets and worked through progressively bigger and nearly always questionable deals. Many have money that far outstrip their level of culture—and some are highly conscious of that fact. Several glossy lifestyle magazines now pitch articles on etiquette to the new moneyed classes.

Russia has little business heritage to draw from and the New Russians' flashy displays of wealth have begun to shape a specific business culture. It emphasizes the "dirty" huge, short-term earnings over "clean" long-term gains, selling not manufacturing, spending not investing and settling business disputes with intimidation or even violence. The New Russians comprise a small but enormously influential sector of Russian business.

Seeking the badges of the wealthy class, the average young Russian consumer is beginning to develop demanding tastes. Russian food products are not good enough; imported products are, to him, the best. Any blue jeans will not do; only those that are top-quality Levi's are good enough. In business, Russians may insist on the best with little regard for cost effectiveness. Equipment far in excess of requirements may be purchased, and state-of-the-art computers may be deemed necessary when current technology will do the job. The accent is on big as beautiful, the more luxurious the better.

Free Market Concepts

Russia's business world has been in limbo since 1917. Basic business concepts familiar to people the world over may be new or totally unknown to Russians. Important contracts may be written without *force majure* clauses, lease-with-the-option-to-buy offers may arouse suspicion, and business maxims like "more reward equals more risk" are barely understood.

The word *mortgage* is listed in a Russian-English dictionary as *ipotyeka* or *zakladnaya*. The first word would not be understood by most Russians and the second is an obsolete word dating back to pre-Revolutionary times. The average Russian has never had a mortgage, doesn't have one now, and is not likely to have one in the future as the state gives ownership of apartments to those who are registered to occupy them.

Most Russians apartments, cars and other possessions remain totally uninsured. Personal insurance is a new field often poorly understood. Many company directors consider insurance a waste of money, and those who do take out policies have no experience with excesses, no-claims bonuses or risk assessment. Some of the new insurance companies initially issued policies far more generous than might have been appropriate because of this lack of experience.

Of course there are Russians with MBA degrees from universities abroad. They and many others would have no trouble explaining a mortgage or concluding an insurance policy. But many business notions are new and are only penetrating the business community gradually, as the market matures.

The Endless Bull Market

Russians don't know the bear market. Business is new and so far the exhilarating roller coaster ride has been only up. Business empires are being created based on ever upward-pointing graphs. Russian businesspeople have never experienced the cycles of boom and bust that are familiar internationally. They were brought up in times that may have been austere by international standards, but were always stable.

There is an easy-come, easy-go attitude toward money, a boom mentality. Inexperienced business players are operating in an underserviced market where competition can be minimal or nonexistent for new ventures. Moreover, wages are rising, disposable incomes are high and start-up costs are still relatively low.

Although there are failures, tens of thousands of firms prosper in conditions that few realize can only be transitory. Many companies are undercapitalized and overextended, though few would recognize either concept. Sometimes fortunes are made, but managing risk is an undeveloped skill. Often companies are staked on single, high-risk deals. Few plan for the day when the bear must come to Russia. A mere stabilization of existing economic growth could likely throw a great number of Russian firms out of business.

The Fast Buck

In the early stages of Russia's transition to a free market system, a thriving trading economy has appeared. The vast majority of all business involves buying in one place and selling in another. Trade in imported goods is fueled by a buying public traditionally starved of foreign goods and dissatisfied with irregular supplies of Russian-made goods they consider inferior. Some estimates put the total value of all such trade in billions of dollars.

Big cities are full of *chyelnoki* (shuttlers), individuals who constantly shuttle back and forth between Russia and Turkey, China, Poland and other low-cost countries. Arriving by plane, train, car or on foot, *chyelnoki* fill their bags with cheap clothes, food products, shoes and electronic goods, which they resell to wholesalers or at markets in Russia. Those who don't have the resources to leave Russia trade within it. Train and subway stations in St. Petersburg and Moscow are filled with Russians, mainly retirees living on meager pensions, who stand holding a few items for sale to passersby. These small-scale traders are symptomatic of what takes place across the country: the movement of goods from one place to another with value added en route.

Many of the street sellers are pushed to sell by necessity. Everybody seems to know a diplomaed engineer who is selling chocolate from a kiosk. But generally, making a fast buck is at the core of present Russian business mentality. Given the prevailing conditions it is easier to make money in the short term by buying and selling rather than actually producing things. The result is an overwhelming concentration on trading—particularly of imported goods—rather than home-based manufacturing, a situation that seems likely to be the case for some time to come.

The trading base is linked to a nationwide fast buck fever. A notorious example was the Moscow-based MMM Invest company. MMM offered very high returns to Russians who bought its shares. Television ads comically portrayed common people striking it rich through an MMM investment and buying long-held desires with ease. Millions poured money into the fund as Russians from all over the country expected to get rich. But MMM turned out to be a massive pyramid scheme that collapsed dramatically, spotlighting the extent of Russia's get-rich-quick attitude.

Robust trading activity has attracted many foreign importers. But they must deal with fickle and severe import taxes. Foreign automobile dealerships doing brisk business in Russia were shocked in early 1994 when the government imposed a 100 percent plus import tax on foreign cars. Food importers face varying complex taxes on different items. Moreover, anytime goods cross a border, customs imposes layers of taxes, fees and often bribes, according to foreign businessmen.

The New Russian Company

Today two kinds of Russian companies predominate. The first, the old, enormous state-run enterprises—mainly factories which produced for the military—face the complicated task of so-called defense conversion. A typical conversion scheme involves a foreign company which negotiates for a modest piece of factory space to form a joint venture and begin an experiment in manufacturing. Kirovsky Zavod in St. Petersburg, for example, has converted a small wing of its expansive complex into a wheelchair manufacturing line which supplies the United Nations. Another wing is a joint venture with U.S.-based heavy equipment maker Caterpillar Inc., which produces frames for excavators. But a major problem for the state-run factories is their size. Most employ tens of thousands of people and must support loss-making employee services, such as kindergartens and shops, without government help. Furthermore, only a small portion of the huge complex undergoes conversion. The state enterprises also tend to have defiantly resistant management at the top who cling to their old power base and resist change.

The second type of company is the small, nimble firm that has proliferated around the country. Most are trading houses or service operations consisting of less than five employees. Trading houses often import electronic goods, food or clothes and resell them out of small shops in big cities. Sometimes a foreign partner is involved. Widespread across Russia is the kiosk, a small, enclosed metal shed from which goods are sold. Many small businessmen own these kiosks, which ideally serve as the forerunner to the shop. As for services, popular industries include advertising and real estate.

A third level of Russian business exists in a thriving underground economy, although no one knows exactly how big it is. These "companies" are generally one or two persons providing goods or services without official business registration, without paying taxes and often working from home. Some deal in illicit goods, some do not. Examples include sales of clone computers, weapons, secondhand cars bought in the West, Russian language instruction and translation, repair of televisions and other electronic equipment. Many of these businesses are simply one individual with an area of expertise. He or she may work officially at a state-run enterprise and receive little pay; the entrepreneurial effort—without being taxed—provides needed financial support.

Business Without a Cash Flow

A Russian semiconductor manufacturer receives a sorely needed $1 million order from a Hong Kong company. Payment will be made upon delivery of semiconductor chips of satisfactory quality. But to implement the order—to buy raw materials like copper and pay for services such as electricity—the company must have some operating capital.

The company director goes to a Russian bank, where he learns of the time-consuming process for a loan application, which, if approved, carries 150 percent interest. The director has few choices. He can turn to loans from the Mafia, which are quick, but dangerous and nearly as expensive. Frustrated, he appeals to the Hong Kong company, which refuses to give a percentage of payment in advance because of general uncertainties of doing business with Russia. Lacking money, the director must reject the order which could have infused his factory with a new life.

This situation is increasingly typical for many Russian companies that have been cut off from government credits. Russian companies offer acceptable products for export, but it's the rare few that can actually manage to sell them.

Russian companies which import products often try to get the goods on credit from the foreign partner, effectively offering consignment sales in Russia.

If an importer does get a loan and the shipment is delayed, high interest accumulates, wiping out any profit. Speed is essential. For example, transportation presents a special problem. Asian companies can sell low-cost products to Russian companies. But Russian companies who have obtained high-interest loans cannot wait the one to two months for delivery by boat. As a result, Russian companies buy Asian goods in Europe at a higher price. Delivery by truck from Europe is much faster, enabling the company to turn over the products faster and quickly repay the loan.

Russian Businesswomen

The cleaning lady at a foreign firm gingerly requested a three-month absence, offering her mother as a replacement. She explained to the foreign manager that her background was actually in aeronautical engineering, and some temporary work involving the launch of satellites in Kazhakstan had become available.

Russia's transition from a military to civilian economy, where issuing directives and controlling money and people outweigh educational achievements, has proved hard for all Russians. Many highly educated people who previously used their talents for Soviet military supremacy have lost prestige and were forced into unskilled labor. Women represent half the workforce and 90 percent of the unemployed.

Women can be found in top jobs in science and the arts. But in business, a woman in a key position is rare. Despite decades of rhetoric extolling men and women as equals, Russia remains a strictly male-dominated culture.

Men are expected to be strong and intelligent, to bring home money, make decisions and generally support their spouse. Women are allowed to seek higher education and enter the workforce, but progress typically halts there. Men dominate leadership positions even more so than in the West.

Yet foreign businesspeople share a consensus that Russian women managers tend to approach work more seriously, display more initiative and work harder than their male counterparts. Unfortunately, women's managerial talents are squandered at a time when they are sorely needed to enhance Russia's nascent managerial class. In new Russian businesses, women play the role of the decoration, "to make the men look more important" as one Russian woman put it. The more cars, mobile phones and beautiful women a firm has, the more impressive it is.

Connections help block the progress of women in business. Most business connections are based on a male network. For Russian women, that brotherhood is practically impossible to crack. And because the Russian culture instills a dependency on men, women are unlikely to form effective networks themselves.

Much more so than in the West, men form the rules of business. Women who do succeed abide by men's rules. Sex appeal could influence a Russian. One foreign businesswoman said: "If you are not willing or able to use that, you are not going to get anywhere." She said men are often keen to sign contracts with women who are prepared to play up sex appeal. "It will not make them ignore major points," she said, "but it will help them overlook things." But she advised an aloof approach. Going too far creates the image of an "easy woman," leading to a loss of respect.

Russians tend to label a woman who achieves success on the job as manly. Indeed, the few successful Russian business-women have had to be tenacious, ruthless and unafraid to confront threats to their power, lending some validity to the stereotype of the warrior woman. To Russians, ambitious women somehow lose their femininity. One foreign woman manager was told she was too good at her job to be a "real woman." She said Russian men find it hard to accept that a woman could excel in both business and at home—in the kitchen and in bed.

Further, Russian women who have moved into power positions often do not have the influence or autonomy a man would have given the same power. If a women is admired as a manager, she may initially be treated with tolerance—though not equality.

Russian women rarely complain of inequality, while foreign women inevitably discuss the Russian woman's inferior status.

Social groups fighting against chauvinism are few and unpopular, suggesting that Russia's ingrained cultural beliefs will remain for some time.

Foreign Women

An equality between the sexes hasn't developed in Russia. Men are masculine and women are feminine in the traditional sense, an attitude potentially offensive to a businesswoman from the West.

Foreign women supervising Russian men may encounter difficulties. Generally, the Russian man deeply resents control by a woman manager. One British businesswoman who has lived six years in Russia said that it is inevitable visiting businesswomen will be treated differently than men, though perhaps not as severely as Russian women. But the foreign businesswoman should not be put off by hand kissing, door opening and flower giving, which is a cultural practice intended to show respect.

Westernized Russian men will be more willing to deal with women. But an older or more conservative businessman may feel the foreign woman can only be a low-level company official. He may feel he has been sold short; in his experience a woman cannot sign on the dotted line without consulting a higher male authority.

In Russia, women in business will probably benefit by displaying a conservative, neat appearance and serious behavior. If heads must roll, she should not be afraid to make them roll. Men respect the woman manager who does what she says, according to one foreign woman. A woman manager pulling back on promises or vacillating on decisions immediately opens herself to confrontation.

Moreover, a certain aloofness, rather than being too friendly, wins more respect. The woman opting to be one of the boys, drinking and carousing with the men after hours is playing a hazardous game. The Russian man will likely interpret female camaraderie as promiscuity and could act according to his passions, with the full sanction of his colleagues.

Finally, relaxed and confident behavior, as if totally unaware that unequal treatment of the sexes could exist in the workplace, will help. Provocative appearance or behavior will cast a woman into the decorative, second-rate category.

Manufacturing

The Russian government has not seriously courted manufacturing operations. Currently there are no government incentives such as tax holidays, land and property discounts and swift registration for foreign companies who want to set up manufacturing. Commentators speculate that the government intentionally keeps manufacturers out to prevent social unrest: Russia's factory-based economy, employing the bulk of the workforce, could be forced into closure by competition, creating bitterness and mass unemployment.

Meanwhile, barriers to entry are growing. Companies which went ahead and set up operations anyway will presumably reap great advantage over competitors. Labor is cheap, plentiful and educated, and a local operation cuts down significantly on notoriously high import taxes. Some manufacturers in Russia include Caterpillar, Coca-Cola, Tambrands Inc., Gillette, Mars, and Procter & Gamble.

Manufacturing operations, according to foreign businesspeople, must initially be controlled by the foreign partner in nearly every stage of production. Suppliers, both local and foreign, usually cannot be relied upon. Various infrastructure problems, such as transportation and telecommunications, and other factors, such as work stoppages, equipment breakdowns and continuously changing laws and taxes, make quality and delivery of supplies inconsistent. So the small number of manufacturing operations with foreign partners often follow closely the vertically integrated model common to Western industries of the past. McDonald's fast food chain, for example, grows its own produce and runs its own beef slaughterhouse.

Nearly 80 percent of Russia's industries are privatized and foreign manufacturers have typically bought their existing operations. Building a plant on a so-called green field site is costly and construction can be lengthy. But buying an existing factory presents its own problems. Most plants need a complete equipment upgrade or overhaul. Padded staff is one of the most complex problems. Russian workers want a foreign owner because to them it means security. But they also know that mass dismissals will be imminent. If the employees hold the privatization shares in the factory, retaining staff is a key negotiating point when a foreign partner wants to buy the plant.

Finally, foreign manufacturers have one recommendation learned from the school of hard knocks. If buying into a factory, make sure the purchase is for the entire factory, not part of it. If a foreign company buys a section of a factory, and their business reaps profit while the rest of the factory faces hard times, the foreign company will end up paying for all electricity, power, water, etc. They'll be supporting dead wood. Moreover, when the other side sees employees of the foreign company are treated relatively well, using good equipment and earning better salaries, envy will likely grow. Envy is a strong and troublesome force in Russia.

End Running the Law

A Russian factory sells $1 million in copper, payable in hard currency, to a European partner. After the contract is inked, the Russian factory manager calls the Western partner and tells him to deem the copper shipment of inferior quality upon its arrival in the European port. Accept the shipment, but file documents validating the metal's poor quality and mail them back to Russia. There is nothing wrong with the copper. But if the European partner cooperates, he will be billed only 90 percent of the copper's value. The Russian partner then turns to its Russian supplier, shows the documents of inferior quality, and therefore is only required to pay 80 percent of the price to the supplier. The factory manager makes $100,000 in tax-free money, the European partner has a $100,000 discount and the supplier is so happy to receive hard currency for his materials that no suspicions arise. Everyone is happy.

This example is one variation of a multitude of clever ways that Russians do an end run on the law and benefit themselves. In the West, every step of a business deal is formalized and fixed by written law. But in Russia, literal adherence to the written word—rules, contracts, laws—does not have the importance that it does in the West. Russians have more flexibility with written documents, which are seen as loose agreements.

Moreover, Russians have an inclination to do things *na lyeva* ("on the left"), or in nonofficial ways. It is a legacy of the old system in which the official way meant bureaucratic snags, the runaround and an interminable amount of waiting. In addition, Russian society views personal connections and the ability to take care of friends as important status symbols and these characteristics are encouraged. Managers will strike deals with bureaucrats and other official authorities, such as customs officers, to create mutually profitable business deals. *Ruka ruky moiyet* ("One hand washes the other") is used in an envious and sometimes cynical sense to describe others' obvious use of personal connections strictly for mutual benefit of the parties involved.

Despite the constant introduction of various business laws, the mentality remains. One area where it is strong, and where the post-Soviet system has gotten worse rather than better, is tax law. Cheating on taxes is rampant and endemic is Russia. Some businesspeople admit to evading taxes simply for increased profit.

The foreign visitor should not be shocked by influence transactions or manipulation of the law, which would typically be condemned as unabashed corruption in the West. A nascent legal system, absence of fundamental business ethics and a culture based on patronage makes such practices endemic in Russia's newly emerging free market system.

9
TODAY'S RUSSIAN EMPLOYEE

Russians In the Foreign Workplace

Russians will view the foreign company as a highly desirable place to work. In the Russian view, foreign companies don't go bankrupt because they pay their employees as promised, are run efficiently and use modern equipment. Perquisites include business trips abroad, exposure to international market practices, and a salary pegged to the dollar to guard against inflation.

One foreign company wanted to pay salaries in dollars as an attractive perk for Russian employees, but Russian law forbids hard currency salaries. Management bypassed the law by issuing employees American Express cards with a spending limit corresponding to their wages. These stories get around and Russians are influenced by them.

But when Russians see that they must work hard and long for a small salary, they may decide to leave. Work at a Russian company, where the salary is nearly the same but work is far less, could be the better choice. In fact, some parts of the workforce would rather return to the old centrally planned system where they barely had to work at all until December, when the factories would run double shifts to meet year-end production targets.

Work Is Like Home

Russian employees see the workplace as a second home and many expect their bosses and colleagues to be knitted into their personal lives. That could mean lending the company car for an employee wedding, providing small gifts for birthdays and other celebrations, or sympathetically tolerating tardiness or time off if a family member is ill or a difficult situation exists at home. The boss may have to accept that an employee will go away for four weeks to care for a sick grandparent in the village. Above all, the foreign manager will likely learn about employees' families, as they reveal their private lives.

It's also common for employers to provide free or generously subsidized meals to employees during the day, to pay for their monthly transportation ticket and offer other benefits. The Soviet workplace has a strong tradition of employee benefits such as inexpensive *stolovaye* (cafeterias), day care centers, subsidized housing and transportation.

If work relationships are close, Russian employees believe it is necessary to meet socially with their colleagues. Management should invite other managers to dinner, for example. Neglect of this small gesture can damage relationships, with the foreigner being seen as cold and uncaring.

Getting drunk and carousing with colleagues is going too far and can be disastrous. Any improprieties can be fed into the gossip machine or can be used against the foreign boss in the future. Knowing how far to go is essential.

Workplace Gossip

For seventy years, the safest way to exchange information was by word of mouth. If some major development happened in Moscow, Russians in the outlying cities would know about it by coded telephone talk or travelers carrying news.

Russians have strong oral traditions. The average person has polished verbal skills and can gossip very well. The foreign manager will probably be overwhelmed with the amount of rumors and personal chatter in the workplace. Gossip should be ignored, even if it is true.

Attitude Toward the Company

Many foreign companies enter Russia with the illusion that their employees will be enthused by the thought of working with a company with a proud tradition and household name abroad. Russian employees' loyalties are usually directed at a lower level—often with the local manager rather than the company image.

Russians have a difficult time identifying themselves with the company as it has not been part of their work ethic. It was difficult for workers to feel an enthusiastic sense of belonging to anonymous workplaces with names like Meat Factory #724 or Hospital #1.

There is also a question of responsibility. It is considered the bosses' responsibility to take care of the company, not the workers'. Russian workers, especially in newly privatized industries with a lifetime of state patronage and monopoly behind them, find too abstract any idea that their livelihood depends on their performance. They have no notion that the company's success or failure relies on them as much as management.

The Russian employee's loyalty can either be nonexistent, with money the only motivation and the job seen just as a stepping stone, or it can be intense, with the employee loving the product and worshipping the boss. In the latter case affection for the job normally withers if the boss leaves. There doesn't seem to be much of a middle ground.

Work Registration

Every Russian is registered both at their place of abode and place of work. The work registration comes in the form of a *trudavaya knyeshka* (labor book), which is held by the employer and contains the person's work history: the places and dates of past employment and previous positions held with a description of the role. There is also a special section for rewards such as medals for exemplary labor. In Soviet times police would check documents and penalize those without work.

Not being officially registered at a workplace for more than a month can have severe consequences. A pension could be adversely affected by periods without work. Today many Russians are officially registered as employees in state enterprises that are teetering on bankruptcy. There is little or no work to be done, so the employees stay home or even work at another job, returning to the factory occasionally to collect a small salary. Nobody wants to officially sever connections with their existing job until they are certain of a new position in another company.

Hiring

Under the Soviet system, citizens did not find work by answering newspaper advertisements or applying to an employment agency. Job vacancies were plentiful. For the laborer, nearly every factory had openings. For the university graduate, government placement in a job was guaranteed. Personal connections and Communist Party membership also played a large role in getting a highly desired job and location.

Because no competitive labor market existed, resumes, help wanted ads and the concept of "selling oneself" to a prospective employer are new phenomena in Russia. A company that advertises for a professional employee, listing the skills required, may get responses from hundreds of people not even remotely suitable, but all saying that if only given a chance they would be great at the job. Therefore, advertisements must be worded specifically, emphasizing that only those with the required skills should apply.

Typically, friends of those already employed at a company will be encouraged to apply. An employer should be aware that too many friends of friends could possibly turn the company into a highly politicized workplace, with employees broken up into factions and spending too much energy spreading gossip.

Top-notch managers can be found in Russia despite the rigid conditioning of the inefficient state system. Most successful joint ventures have begun initially with strong foreign management which carefully controls the operation while simultaneously training selected Russian managers. Eventually, the Russian managers will be expected to run the business. McDonald's Corporation in Moscow, for example, employs tens of thousands of people yet only three top managers are non-Russian and soon even they are expected to be replaced by locals.

Russian Managers

Russian managers who grew up in the Soviet system share some general characteristics. Usually they want to have many soldiers under them. Typical in a state-run enterprise was an assortment of managers with titles such as chief vice director, vice director, assistant vice director, deputy vice director, etc. Moreover, managers had no philosophy about cutting costs. Even today, despite the bad financial situation of their company, they don't try to find and trim inefficiencies. Instead, managers tend to focus solely on the production end, trying to make production more profitable.

When selecting a Russian manager, foreign businesspeople say the ability to speak English does not matter. They feel that practical sensibilities are more important. Does the person give a direct answer rather than digress? Many retain an old authoritative habit of answering a question with a question, which cuts off dialogue. Is the manager willing to entertain new ideas? There is a category of people in Russia who are unable to accept change. The top Russians who will run the operations also should not be simultaneously involved in other companies. Many are, and attention and energy are diverted from their main jobs.

Firing

Firing an employee is an extremely delicate issue in Russia. Since no competitive labor market existed and full employment of all able-bodied citizens was guaranteed by the government, firing was a rare occurrence. If an employee was dismissed, lack of professional competence was seldom the reason. Usually a political transgression was involved. Managers were interested in ensuring that nobody did or said anything that would drop them in political hot water and affect their party career path. Other causes for redundancy were that the boss wanted to make room to move in his own friends, or that the employee had severely strained the relationship with his boss. But essentially, the Soviet citizen who kept away from politics was never fired.

If an employee was to be fired, it was normal to ask for a

resignation letter to avoid Soviet labor law complications. In fact, it was considered a favor to an outgoing employee to be allowed to resign and give the appearance of voluntarily leaving for another position, because the article of the law under which an employee left (i.e., voluntarily or forcible) would be stamped in his personal labor book. Getting another job could be extremely difficult for those marked down as having been fired—sometimes they even attempted to bribe their bosses to allow them to resign instead.

Today the average Russian views employment in a foreign company as secure compared to a job at a Russian firm. Foreign managers should keep in mind that the practice of firing has always been rare and Russians are not used it. An employee does not hold lingering uncertainty about his position once hired; he expects to remain at the job until he decides to change. Therefore, a fired Russian employee will often feel a deep sense of humiliation and personal slight, much more so than an employee in the West, who understands that being fired is a part of life. Firing decisions should be undertaken only as a last resort, and only after elaborate measures have been taken to ease the burden of the employee involved.

Time

All of Russia seems to be running at a tangibly slower pace than in the West. Moscow may have an energy to it, but a slow energy. Other large cities, however, still close their shops for an hour during lunch, take frequent breaks and chat a lot between customers. In the morning, management typically floats into the office after ten o'clock. The Russian workaholic is rare. In fact, a person in a hurry is often seen as impolite or disrespectful.

Russia's antiquated infrastructure, the casual attitudes of most Russians and a general atmosphere of unpredictability create an unofficial rule about time: Find the most liberal estimate of time to accomplish something, then double it.

In the past, the workforce had no need to be time-conscious and notions of speedy time to market simply didn't exist. Therefore, deadlines have an elasticity that may not be acceptable to foreign businesspeople. Injecting a sense of urgency into production, for example, will require repetitive training stressing the importance of time. A project may fail to meet a deadline because one department finishes its work but doesn't coordinate with other departments to continue the job. Department managers, used to living in a society of endless delays, consider it foolish to hunt down and find the project bottleneck, reasoning nothing can be done about it anyway.

Another reason for incomplete or late work is the difficulty many Russian employees have in prioritizing tasks. They have a problem breaking larger tasks into components and working through them in a logical and consistent way. Russians innately sense the sweep of the big picture, but struggle with or disregard the practical details. They lack practice in incremental steps toward a goal; their tendency has been to dramatically jump from the first to the last step.

Authority: The Boss

Russian employees find it difficult to talk to authority figures. Dissatisfied Russian employees will seldom confront the boss with a request for extra pay or better conditions. Instead they complain to everyone around them—and start to look for another job. Usually, the boss doesn't suspect a problem exists until the employee comes to give notice that he is leaving. In many cases it is only then that problems are tackled.

Western methods of identifying problem areas may fall flat. One foreign manager who introduced the concept of quarterly appraisals into her company said they can be "like pulling teeth. My employees will tell me nothing unless I ask every question three different ways. That takes time and patience."

In general, the boss is seen as an authority figure who makes the critical decisions. Russians do not feel that a boss has to work—in fact a good boss should not work, but simply sit around the office and make decisions.

But there must be a boss. Russian workers expect and create hierarchies. Even if two people are of equal status on the company's management structure charts, they will be secretly ranked by workers. A title or the size of an office or even mere personality could be the determining factor. Those rankings sometimes conflict with the official management structure.

The majority of young, educated Russians, however, may quickly become sensitive to authority as they learn the ropes. One problem foreign managers cite stems from the training process in professional positions. As a Russian employee gains experience and has some successes, he can be offended by strict authority. "Six months after being trained they may believe they are at the level of a person with fifteen or twenty years experience," says one American sales manager. "They start asking for their rights and privileges, comparing themselves to a highly trained Western person. Six months ago, they were afraid of the boss."

Tell Me What To Do

One foreign boss finally realized that the frequent lack of results from his staff stemmed from the way he was giving directions. While statements like "I think we should do this . . ." or "Maybe you should try this . . ." coming from the boss would have been taken as orders in his own culture, they were being received by Russian employees as options—and options they were loathe to try for fear of being blamed if they didn't work. Many Russian employees expect firm commands containing exact directions. They often expect to be told where, when, and how to do a job.

Russians also work according to their job descriptions rather than with some general notion of their role. What a foreign employer means by *secretary* could be very different to what the prospective employee understands by the phrase. Descriptions should be detailed on paper and gone over by the employer and new employee.

Pride in the Job

Most Westerners on the giving or receiving end of a transaction take for granted, at least in theory, that a product or service should be of the highest quality possible given the money and resources devoted to it. Pride may be gained from a job well done. Similar attitudes do not always prevail in Russia.

Soviet Russians spent their entire lives getting around the system. But in Russia "the system" was the government, the workplace and the employer. Attitudes that people in other countries might reserve for the tax department were directed at the system in Russia.

Resourcefulness

When necessary, employees can be incredibly resourceful with technology, producing impressive results with unimpressive tools. Engineers and technicians typically build computers themselves from cheap components or repair equipment on the spot rather than sending it to a specialist.

Technological ingenuity springs from necessity. The Soviet system was infamous for parts shortages of nearly all essential items, from room lamps to automobiles and tractors. Russians often had to jerry-rig machinery (*somopol*) or fashion their own parts. One of the authors recalls a staff photographer who had built a fully functioning color film processing machine from a scrap metal tube, discarded plastic containers and a cheap electric motor—a copy of a complex processing unit that would sell for thousands of dollars in the West.

About Teamwork

Outsiders may misassociate the Soviet idea of the "collective" with the Western idea of "teamwork" or "team spirit." The Soviet work collective was more like an army brigade (some actually bore the name *brigade*). The word defined groups of "workers:" perhaps a class of students, a section in a factory, the staff of a shop.

The collective was a permanent unit rather than a team brought together for a special goal. Big on theory, it did little to foster concrete notions of collective responsibility.

In the Soviet system, responsibility was handed upward, leaving people with little reason to care for the overall result of their labor. How the collective's work fit into the big picture was largely irrelevant. That was the problem of the person at the top. A worker in a collective concentrated solely on his own task at hand. The consequence is sometimes apparent today when Russians try to fit into a team structure or operate in unison with other departments of a company.

Sharing of information within departments, or even between individuals within the same department, is minimal. One member of a team may solve an operational problem that has bugged employees for months—but he may not share the information with the others. Malice is seldom involved. People simply don't grasp the notion that other employees and the company as a whole will benefit by sharing information—or they assume the others will work out the problem as well.

Result Versus Process: Getting the Job Done

In the coal mine, Ukrainian miner Alexei Stakhanov one day turned to a friend and suggested they work the coal face differently. Instead of both men digging and then stopping to hammer supporting beams in to prevent the tunnel from collapsing, Stakhanov would dig and his friend would hammer. The pair exceeded their work norm many times over.

Little did Stakhanov realize that this tiny act would elevate him to the status of a Soviet icon. The Communist media turned Stakhanov into a national hero. Workers across the country began the push for better output. Thousands of typists strove to exceed their twenty-four pages a day, doctors rushed to treat greater numbers of patients, textile workers churned out many more meters of cloth—all labored to exceed their norms and join the ranks of the superhuman *Stakhanovets* workers.

In the frenzy to produce, quality inevitably suffered. Yet eventually production-obsessed authorities increased the norms, reasoning that if a few could produce the higher numbers, then why not many?

But there was a longer lasting legacy. Such attitudes have led to an obsession with results rather than the process by which they are achieved. Energy plus enthusiasm (in former times revolutionary zeal) became more important than the planning, efficiency or details involved in completing a quality job.

Planning tends to be extremely short term or even nonexistent. Neglected details add up and throw what plans do exist into confusion. Lack of a coherent strategy results in impressive energy wasted to achieve goals that even elementary analysis would have indicated were of marginal or no benefit.

Unions

The Soviet Union was the land of the worker. *Soviet* translates literally as "council." Workers' unions had been allowed little chance to develop under the czarist regime, and with the advent of the Soviet workers' paradise they were clearly redundant. Organizations bearing the name of "Union" abounded, and still do, but few if any were true workers' organizations agitating for improved conditions, rights and wages for worker members. That function had, in theory, been taken on by the benevolent government. Unions became formalized arms of government.

Today Russia is virtually bereft of unions as they are known in the West, though it does have a complex and comprehensive body of legislation dealing with workers and working conditions in a decidedly favorable way. Russia had no nationwide mass strikes which would have demobilized the country after the collapse of the Soviet Union. However, workers are showing marked solidarity in demanding higher wages and benefits from a government which has chosen to stop supporting ailing industries.

Technology

Cold War secrecy, immense bureaucracy and a lack of cash are among the reasons Russia failed to keep up with world trends in technology. Every service and industry suffered. Oil companies are using antiquated machinery, making drilling grossly inefficient. The multitude of government agencies lacked computers and mountains of paperwork piled up, thickening the already clogged system. Newspapers were limited in length because no page inserting machines were available—the inserting work was done by hand.

Foreigners walking into Soviet offices in the 1980s often felt as if they had stepped back thirty years in time. Not a computer, but a rotary telephone sat on the desk. To make an international phone call, a three-day reservation was required and even then circuits may have been busy. They had no facsimile or photocopying machines.

Technology is being upgraded slowly. Foreign high technology companies are doing brisk business in Russia, installing optical fiber cable, paging, cellular and digital switching networks, selling in volume modern phone systems, computers and office automation equipment. Moscow and St. Petersburg are modernizing the fastest and many small Russian businesses today have at least one computer. But the rest of the vast country is only slowly entering the modern technological age.

10
DEALING WITH RUSSIANS

Protocal for Meetings

Meetings must be face-to-face; the telephone is used only to set the time and place. On arrival, the Westerner should shake hands firmly and look his Russian acquaintances in the eyes. When meeting someone new, Russians want to look into the person's eyes. Eye contact is also important when speaking.

Russians are not habitually punctual, but the foreign businessperson should be on time. In Russia, always allow twenty to thirty minutes when waiting for someone to arrive. Expect smoking. If the foreign visitor smokes or has coffee or tea, he should always first offer the same to Russians. Russians tend to believe clothes are important at the first negotiation with a Westerner. In later negotiations, a polished appearance is of less importance. The exchange of business cards is gaining importance. The card is often left on the table in front of the person who received it until the meeting finishes.

Meetings with management of state enterprises are usually dour affairs, without humor, graphic wizardry or a clear agenda, although the situation is slowly changing. Soviet Russia created a culture in which meetings were held out of habit, without clear objectives or direction.

Furthermore, most meetings are characterized by digressions and a status-conscious atmosphere. It is common to walk into meetings and find several people in the room who you do not know and whose function or status is never explained. It is necessary to identify the Russian in charge and pay him due respect by directing key points to him. Addressing his subordinate with important issues may offend him.

Another possible protocol debacle concerns language. Many Russians have studied English but have no practice in speaking it. Generations of students entered the workforce able to read the language but with a poor command of spoken English. Today a Russian businessman may speak through an interpreter because he can't express himself adequately in spoken English and feels embarrassed to reveal it. Therefore if a Russian is with an interpreter, it doesn't necessarily mean he has no familiarity with English.

Similarly, during meetings the foreigner should be wary when conducting conversation among colleagues in a foreign language. The Russian language has borrowed thousands of words from English, French, German and other languages. Words like *ambition, prostitute, bank, manager, tradition* and *revolution,* to name a few, are identical or very similar in their Russian forms. Keep comments confidential to avoid embarrassing situations.

Talking Business: Smooth Communication

The visitor who believes he has a tacit understanding with a Russian should be careful of misunderstandings. The language of Dostoyevsky, Pushkin and Chekov is proliferous and abstract and Russians love to play with words. Even a cursory study of the language reveals the incredible size of vocabulary. Despite the number of available words, delivering nuances in Russian is difficult. For a sentence to carry an intended impact the words must be clearer and more concrete than in English. Implication must be much more apparent, since subtle innuendo and understatement will normally pass unrecognized.

The Russian conversational method tends to follow a specific pattern. Russians don't usually jump from topic to topic quickly and superficially like many Westerners do. They tend to stick with one topic, cover it thoroughly, then use obvious transitions to change to another subject. Those unaware of this conversational rule are likely to open the door to general confusion.

Soured relationships resulting from misunderstandings seem to be commonplace. A foreigner who speaks a little Russian meeting with a Russian who speaks a little English may each believe they understand each other. In fact this assumption is fertile ground for error. Russian contains words that masquerade as their English equivalent. The Russian word *magazin* does not mean magazine but "shop;" *akkuratno*, which sounds like the English "accurate," usually means "neatly." Only the experienced and fluent foreign speaker of Russian should forgo hiring an interpreter.

Because of the language's abstractness, foreigners who have business meetings with Russians should be prepared. Questions that do not demand specific answers will likely result in lengthy, vague explanation and digressions. To avoid drifting from the point of the discussion, a foreigner should try to use concrete examples in questions. For example, instead of asking, "What are the characteristics of the Russian market?", a better worded question would be, "Our company sold one-half million boxes of Brand X detergent in Moscow during 1994. In 1995 we want to double sales in the city. If you were in our situation, what would be your specific recommendations?"

Of course, lengthy digressions may be performed in the best tradition of *pohkazuka*, concealing ignorance of the subject under discussion. It may be the twentieth time the foreign party has negotiated for the rights to a foreign offshore oil field—but likely the first time the Russians have sold one. They don't know the procedure, the international business protocol, what documents they should produce, or perhaps even the market value of their assets—but they are not going to admit it. In fact, some argue that Russians have an instinctive aversion to admitting their shortcomings in front of foreigners.

Negotiations with Russians

Proud, serious, authoritative, the director of a Soviet enterprise told the team of foreign businessmen seated before him the history of his large factory. It had been the biggest producer of machine parts in the former Soviet Union. It had a sterling reputation, earning repeated awards for reaching production quotas. It had been personally visited by Khrushchev and Brezhnev, and parts from his factory had been used in the space program. Russians across the country knew of his factory. His four-point business plan was quickly explained by touching each of his fingertips.

His attitude, recalls Alexander Sapozhnikov, director of Image Alpha Consulting in Moscow, "is that you must invest in us because of our great reputation, which can only mean great things to come. The foreign side, of course, didn't see it that way."

Russian enterprises do indeed have a lot to offer, but many directors of such enterprises still expect their past triumphs to play a key role in today's business. A director of a large state-run enterprise did not get to his position by being humble, modest or flexible. There is no reason to expect him to offer or understand reasonable, long-term arrangements with a foreign partner.

When faced with such a situation, the foreign businessperson can begin by showing thoughtful respect for the factory and past accomplishments. For example, knowing some of the history of the enterprise may soothe the director's ego.

Still, no matter how adroitly the director's power base is acknowledged, top-level negotiations involving enterprise directors, officials or politicians invariably hinge upon what rewards the Russian principles will receive for themselves. Because of his high position and his potential to yield power, the Russian principle will likely feel he deserves to be rewarded personally for his efforts. This often includes a cash sum, shares of foreign stock or other monetary gifts.

Therefore, a foreigner who only details long-term benefits is put at a disadvantage. Russia's dynamic and volatile environment leaves few Russians holding a strong belief in tomorrow's benefits. A proposed partnership, for example, could stress long-term benefits but hold out short-term payoffs to the primary persons involved.

Trade negotiations with smaller companies run differently, according to foreign businesspeople. Russians in trade negotiations lack the shrewdness of their free-market-oriented counterparts. The situation is slowly changing as more Russians catch on to subtly persuasive sales techniques. But the small store or company will still respect a foreigner. "They're not used to foreigners visiting them," recalls one foreign sales representative for a large Western company. "If a foreigner goes to a small shop or company, they have the upper hand. They still treat you with respect, as if you know something they don't [in terms of business]. There is still an inferiority complex in terms of trading, not as individuals but as a whole."

Navigating Through Negotiations

Thousands of years of toiling and suffering under the ruling elite has conditioned the psyche of Russians. They often see negotiating as a zero-sum game. That is, one side cannot win without the other side losing. A win-win situation, alien to their past experience, will need emphasis and clear explanation.

A struggle to come to an agreement is nearly expected. Lack of free market knowledge, the reluctance to admit it and inexperience with compromise can tie up the most mutually attractive deal.

The foreign negotiator will likely gain advantage by being polite but tough and unwavering, an approach generally respected in Russia. Giving something right away or too fast makes Russians suspicious. Often they must feel as if they have won their concessions. An opposing side with a conciliatory posture can also arouse the domineering character of Russians. Spotting weakness, the latent dictator appears and tries to push the potential partner into submission.

But Russians are obstinate and forceful negotiators only to a point. Many will respond to reason when faced with persistent logical arguments. Wearing down an illogical argument by insisting on a logical approach may work well. However, the foreign businessperson must keep in mind that Russians should be allowed to retreat from their position without loss of face.

Negotiating goals are often vague. Soviet business meetings were usually held for form's sake, without clear objectives or direction. An inordinate amount of time can be spent discussing details before a broad agreement in principle has been reached. Inexperience can also be the reason for not getting down to business. Lack of free market knowledge and the reluctance to lose face by admitting it can tie up negotiations.

Another area of business talks that deserves special attention involves figures. Heads of Russian companies generally don't understand the concept of a business plan, even though they're looking for foreign investment. They are unfamiliar with Western ways of calculating production costs. The new Russian businesspeople can be especially weak in this area. Therefore, figures from the Russian side may sometimes seem unusual. A good practice is to recheck figures and the assumptions used to generate them. The Russian phrase *vzyat s potolka* ("to take from the ceiling") equates with the English "out of thin air." Many business figures are arrived at in this way.

Special care must be taken when the foreign side submits financial estimates and projections. On a day-to-day level, price haggling is barely understood and rarely practiced in Russia. The state always set every price, whether for a bag of flour or a car—and the price was about the same in every shop across eleven time zones. Often Western negotiators put figures on the table, which the Russian side rejects as too high or too low. No counterproposal is made. Moreover, the Russian side may assume the other side is locked into a set of figures once they are proposed.

If a foreign company invites Russian companies to bid on a project, price quotes can range wildly. More often, however, a small company director tends to ask "How much will you pay me?" rather than suggesting a figure himself.

Foreigners should also be aware of a hidden agenda. If in the West money has equaled power, in Soviet Russia power equaled money. The Russian party at the negotiating table may value the power resulting from the deal as much as the profit in the forecasts. But power can't really be quantified and it may hang above the discussion unstated by the Russian side and unnoticed by the foreign side.

Finally, the foreign negotiator should keep in mind the value of having Russians on the negotiating team as advisors. Foreign companies in Russia tend to rely on their own internal experts who are often unequipped to keep up with the rapidly changing laws. A blend of Russians and foreigners can mitigate the "us versus them" atmosphere, which is instinctively felt by Russians when dealing with foreigners. Moreover, Russians who work for foreign companies can often guide their colleagues through communication difficulties and more accurately discern the feeling on the Russian side.

Red Dictators and Yes Men

Two common character types the foreign businessperson may encounter in negotiations with Russians are the *Yes Man* and the *Red Dictator*.

Yes Men tend to agree to everything initially proposed without attempting to secure more favorable terms for their side. The *Yes Men* are usually well intentioned, inexperienced and suffer from unrealistic thinking. In negotiations, such a person will be a delight to the foreign side, which can secure a handsome deal without resistance.

But in the long term, trouble may result from negotiating an unusually attractive deal with a Yes Man. Several businessmen have advised against it. Yes Men have been dealt a crippling blow in philosophy and harbor deep insecurities. The Western partner must cut an equitable slice for the Yes Man that pays off in the long term. Otherwise the seeds of destruction are already sown. As the Russian partner gains more experience, he may feel duped by the initial deal and destroy the partnership.

By contrast, meet the *Red Dictator*. Red Dictators are often older, powerful men involved at senior levels with institutions or with companies that have a viable product. Red Dictators who can change their way of thinking stand a good chance of becoming dollar millionaires by hooking into joint ventures. Those who can't adapt to new market rules simply try to hang on to the last real thing they have—power.

Red Dictators are characterized by their forceful top-down approach. They do the talking, set the terms, dictate the deal. Every step of the way, they are in charge.

A Red Dictator in the St. Petersburg government ushered in a group from Australia for talks on a sports sponsorship project. Instead of two-way negotiations, the Australians got a lecture on exactly what they were required to do. Discussion was not allowed. He then dismissed the group, adding that he was happy there would be future collaboration. His deputy, he said, would sort out the details of the stated project because he had another meeting to attend. The Australians, detailed proposal still in hand, had fallen into quiet resentment. The Russian side had assumed their silence signaled agreement.

The Red Dictator's ideas were commercially unviable and couldn't be challenged, so the Australians went ahead with the project without the Russian partner. Soon they found themselves in a typically Russian situation: the project arrived at a crucial bottleneck, obstructed by the same Red Dictator. If he couldn't run the project, he certainly wasn't going to let anyone else assume control.

Russia is strewn with the wreckage of deals put together by foreigners who thought they could reform Yes Men and Red Dictators. Long-time foreign businesspeople advise against dealing with them if possible. There are many other Russians who do want to do business on a mutually acceptable level.

Sign on the Dotted Line

Foreigners tend to believe that Russians cannot be relied upon to honor contracts. A common complaint relates how a Russian buyer signed a contract to buy goods from a foreign company, then broke the contract when someone else came along with a better offer. Similarly, work contracts don't seem to mean much in Russia. A high-level Russian manager hired to work at a joint venture can casually break his commitment without severe legal penalty.

Certainly Russians view contracts differently. In the West, a written contract is carefully scrutinized to eliminate ambiguity and the document is respected by both parties. In Russia, however, contracts are written and signed without the under-lying premise that either party in violation of what is written will be subject to legal action. In theory, Russian law backs contracts. But penalties for violation are generally lenient and enforcement tends to be lax. Moreover, the legal system is only evolving and Russian contract lawyers lack familiarity and experience with the complex contract laws.

Stories of broken agreements have circulated, fueling deep distrust of written documents. Papers that require Russians to sign on the dotted line hold little credibility among the general population.

Therefore, more emphasis will be placed on the word of the parties to an agreement, which is one reason why face-to-face meetings and close relationships hold great importance.

Partners

The foreigner is armed with statistics, plans a month-long market research project and spends long hours analyzing forecasts and projections. The Russian simply wants to do business. He wants to use his connections and navigate the partner through the complicated system so they can both make a profit. All the paperwork, the Russian will insist, is unnecessary. His attitude is "We do it my way, just trust me." The foreign side sees the Russian as irresponsible and pushy.

According to Oleg Mihailov, a partner in Mihailov-McCloud Consultancy in Moscow, "The Russian typically wants to set up business much faster than the foreign partner. Westerners do extensive research on the business and they don't like unknown quantities." But Russians don't like to deal with business plans and market research. They have their own connections and their own methods of dealing with the government and business associates, which they feel are too complicated and unnecessary to explain.

Despite the clash of approaches, viable, lucrative partnerships are being formed rapidly. Foreign businesspeople, however, should first do thorough background checks on potential partners. Organized crime has set up shell companies, formed foreign partnerships, then taken over the business. Speaking English should not be a requirement to be a good partner, but knowing how to write up a realistic business plan is. The foreigner seeking a Russian partner should emphasize a long-term approach to business. He should posit a conservative initial investment, instill tight company spending policies and insist on initial strong foreign control over the operation—until Russian managers are sufficiently trained to take over.

A step-by-step approach to Russia brings the best possible results.

Joint ventures were the company vehicle of choice when the first large-scale wave of foreign investors headed for Russia in 1991 and 1992. Many early joint ventures were characterized by unrealistic expectations on both sides. The mistakes of that wave have left their mark on the Russian business psyche.

Early foreign partners often poured money into the venture; the Russian side was to supply the local labor and navigation through the Russian system. The foreign side often provided fledgling Russian businesspeople with new cars, flashy offices, computers and cellular phones. With ego sufficiently inflated, the Russian partner would then insist on full control over the business and the venture dissolved. Moreover, there was often confusion about roles such as investor, company director and company owner, as well as frequent ignorance on the Russian side of basic financial principles. Friction inevitably resulted and many joint ventures ended in messy collapse.

Recalls one foreign businessperson who helped set up a joint manufacturing venture in 1991 in Ukraine:

> Foreigners came over for joint ventures. They attracted Soviet partners very easily because the partners knew they would get as much as they could because this joint venture would not work. So a lot of foreigners came over here and registered their JVs [joint ventures] and the partners got what they could, without putting anything in. Soviet partners promised the world because they knew the JV would fail. Then when it failed, they waited for the next one to come along.

Unfulfilled expectations were not limited to Western partners. Often Russian businesspeople found that they had hooked into undercapitalized or unprofessional foreign companies who had underestimated the cost or difficulty of doing business in Russia.

As a basic rule, a joint analysis of expectations and motivation for partnership is vital where the two sides' understanding of the market and of corporate goals is very different. Often orientations clash: the short-term partner and the long-term partner always end up in conflict.

Step by Step

Business in Russia is generally best done step by step. If early meetings go well, that is the time to suggest dinners and family introductions—the bonding that is essential to doing business in Russia. But don't take it too far. Getting unusually drunk with principles to seal a deal has its drawbacks. Russians may have more respect for the foreigner who stays in control. "They want you to show yourself—but later on they may use your antics against you," says one American businessperson.

Likewise with investment. Beginning with a modest approach, escalating the investment and involvement gradually in proportion to the success of the joint venture has proved prudent. For example, when a tentative deal is thrashed out, it is common for foreigners operating in Russia to build "triggers" into the agreement to test for continuing commitment—an early warning system to signal any waning of enthusiasm. A Texan businessperson who has lived seven years in Russia, uses what he calls his "bench-mark system." He divides contracts or tasks into many short-term parts, each its own distinct goal. He doesn't commit to the next stage until the Russian side has come good on the last goal. Set realistic goals and stick to them, he advises.

Connections

"I have a friend in the government who will manipulate the laws to help my business."

That statement Russians often blithely reveal, causing discomfort for foreigners raised in a business culture based on the rule of law. Connections, a visitor may feel, are better kept discreet. But a broadly accepted fact of Soviet life was using connections (*svyazi*) to get things done. Russians see no reason why they should be discreet about their connections today.

Russia has no tradition of business law and ethics and as a result people are encouraged to think of accomplishing things in terms of *svyazi*. Connections will free goods from a customs warehouse in days rather than months, find a supply of widgets during a widget shortage or push a document through the intestines of bureaucracy. Despite the changing business landscape, the personal connections held by a potential partner will directly affect his ability to deliver results.

New Russian businesspeople, impatient with foreigners' need for explanations, are typically reluctant to detail how their connections work. Nonetheless, a Russian will instinctively see any deal in terms of *svyazi*, which may be a reason for proposals that seem unusual to foreigners.

On the personal level, it's safe to say that not much gets done in Russia without *svyazi*. But connections don't always have to be influential persons. When looking for an apartment or a repairperson, information or advice, the easiest, most secure way is by asking Russian friends for help. Chances are they will call other friends who will call other friends and soon a solution arises.

A typical example involves a foreigner who wants to buy a train ticket to a certain city. But lines at the ticket booth are long and tickets will likely be sold out. The foreigner solicits the help of a Russian friend, who telephones his friend, a woman who works at the ticket booth. An agreement is made to sell the ticket to the foreigner when he appears at her window. The foreign visitor need not, and should not, ask questions. Questions imply a lack of trust in the friend. Details have been worked out by the friend and the ticket seller. Their agreement carries a strong responsibility for the friend who offered to help: If something goes wrong, he feels it reflects badly on him. Therefore, the foreign visitor should simply hand over the money and receive the ticket!

Helping friends through connections comes as a pleasure to many Russians. When they lived under the Soviet system and could idle away the day, Russians often spent hours with their friends, solving each others' problems, giving advice and making plans.

Once plugged in, the visitor will be astonished at the size of the personal networks.

Interpreters

Caution in past times has affected interpreters as well. If a foreigner uses a Russian interpreter, he should know that the Russian will instinctively sanitize any unpleasant or challenging words that would be difficult to say to an authority figure.

Moreover, a male interpreter should always be hired to speak to other men and he should preferably be of roughly the same age as the speaker; a younger interpreter is invariably nervous when older men are discussing serious issues. A foreigner should spend some minutes with the interpreter before the meeting going over what will be said. Ask the interpreter to point out any ideas or phrases he feels uncomfortable with.

Allow interpreters to proceed at an easy pace. One typewritten page of English, for example, is longer by a third when rendered into Russian. The same applies to spoken English. English is an economical language but when translated into Russian it tends to be verbose.

Basic business concepts may not be understood by Russians. Spending a few minutes running through key words and concepts with the translator before an important meeting can be worthwhile.

Finally, many Russians have studied English and other languages. Teaching methods during the Soviet era and a complete lack of opportunity to practice by traveling abroad or speaking with foreigners inside the country, tended to produce generations of students who could read a foreign language, but had a very poor command of spoken language.

Bribes

No amount of objectivity will veil the fact that today's Russia is infected with graft and corruption. But the situation has been exaggerated by novice foreign businesspeople lacking international experience. The impression that the foreigner can wine, dine and bribe his way through the ranks of politicians, bureaucrats, customs officials and police is false. Corruption undoubtedly varies by region. Bribes have been indignantly refused by those who are assumed to always take them.

On the other hand, everytime goods cross a border, the chances of officials and organized crime extracting bribes rises dramatically. Ports and customs check points are notorious. Stories like that of the American importer who had to pay $6000 in cash to release a container of goods sitting on a dock in Northern Russia circulate within the business community. Unfortunately, corruption seems to be largely tolerated by both government and business.

On the everyday level, Russians are basically proud and honest people who would take offense if offered a bribe. Also, Russia is the land of gift-giving. A bottle of imported liquor brought for a yawning bureaucrat or chocolates handed to a surly salesclerk are traditional gestures for oiling the wheels when done in good taste.

Foreigners needing compromise with higher authority, however, may be expected to pay bribes. A foreigner who installed a small roof satellite dish was confronted by the manager of the building. "That satellite dish, it's taking a lot of space up there you know," the manager said. He governed the building; the dish was likely seen as a foreign infringement of his territory. Money was not asked for explicitly, but the foreigner understood the best response to keep future relations smooth was a cash bribe.

On a larger scale, one American businessperson who has represented several hotel companies looking to invest in Russia says bribes weakly disguised as assistance regularly land on the bargaining table. Such "sweeteners" include hefty donations to social programs. Rather than a complicated series of behind-the-scenes payoffs to various middlemen, the proposal is made directly to the top people. In this sense, Russia is no different than the majority of other countries, as any seasoned businessperson or politician knows.

Disputes

*All Russians renting flats to foreigners charge rent in dollars. Offi-
cially, it is illegal since all cash transactions must be conducted in
roubles. Also, the rent is received without the knowledge of the tax
department.*

*In one foreigner's dispute, a landlord became emotional and argu-
mentative, demanding kitchen appliances be replaced, even though
their condition was not unusually worn. The foreigner attempted to
reason with her, explaining the concept of "normal wear and tear."
But she was immune to logic, convinced that big money had to be
paid. Finally, he remembered he'd kept signed rent receipts every
month. He promised to turn her in to the tax department, adding that
he held her signed receipts. There would be a large fine, he said. At
the least, there would be an investigation. The problem ended.*

In minor disputes, it is advisable for the foreigner to have
an "ace" in his back pocket. The ace should be the final offer
to resolve the situation, and it should be backed by some sort
of strong persuasion in proportion to the dispute. The ace
should be revealed only after all attempts at reasonable compromise have failed. Promising to turn the matter over to a
higher authority known by both parties, and detailing the
possible consequences, can be effective. Nearly all Russians
will avoid the power of higher authority.

Russians can be an emotional people, lacking the ability
to conduct calm debate. Indeed, Russia has no tradition of
discussions and polemics where the viewpoints of others are
respected. If an argument is unavoidable, Westerners tend to
believe in keeping cool and collected while trying to resolve
it with logic. Russians, however, are inclined to explode with
emotion.

The foreigner caught in a dispute should also be aware of
an old Russian ploy which involves diverting attention from
the main substantive issue to side issues, which are usually
emotional. Insist on discussing only the main dispute. Moreover, when attempting to settle the dispute, several friends
or colleagues should be present with the negotiator to fully
support his position. The mere appearance of a group of
supporters can be highly persuasive.

Giving a Russian many options may lead only to confusion and aggravation. It's best to offer two or three clear and simple resolutions, detailing what is in it for the other person.

Major disputes involving large sums, even in legitimate deals, typically involve the services of organized crime. Foreign businesspeople should know that no court of arbitrage has yet established solid foundations. As a result, it is typical to settle some business disputes by physical force, the threat of physical force, or even with a large-caliber revolver.

Russian businesspeople typically pay for a *krisha* (literally roof, a slang word for protector), usually a security firm or Mafia organization, which will be called in if disputes threaten to escalate. Surprisingly, when the two rival sides each call in their *krisha,* the protectors examine the contract and reach a compromise for the businesspeople. No criminal group wants to fight a messy gang war over a few thousand dollars owed to some small business under its protection.

For debt collection disputes, the *krisha* is called in to extract the money from the debtor initially through nonviolent means. The *krisha* takes a percentage of the money recovered. Comparisons to a legitimate debt collection agency are not unfounded. But the *krisha* operates outside the law and with the promise of violence rather than threat of small claims court.

11
RUSSIA'S NATIONAL TREASURE

Natural Resources: Russia's Economic Pillar

The pillar of Russia's economy is her natural resources: oil, coal, natural gas, metals, precious stones and timber. A staggering 82 percent of Russia's total foreign earnings came from the sale of natural resources in 1994. This figure has inched upwards in recent years and is expected to continue to grow slightly if Russia's industrial production continues to fall. It is certain that this figure will not drop significantly in the next decade.

The export of raw materials is the engine that drives Russia's economy, and no businessperson working with Russia can afford to forget this fact. It is the sale of Russia's natural resources that provides tens of millions of Russians with money to feed themselves in cities where 75 percent of all food products are now imported. The same resources also permit a much smaller number of New Russians to live far beyond the means of successful Western businesspeople.

Moscow tends to wield Russia's natural resources as a political weapon. Many newly independent states remain dependent on Russia's natural resources and all sides know that economic prosperity can only come through cooperation with Russia. Otherwise, those newly independent states risk being left even further behind economically.

Free Natural Resources

Natural resources appear to be grossly unappreciated by the average Russian. A Russian housewife will think nothing of leaving water streaming from the faucet while she answers the telephone and proceeds to talk for fifteen minutes. Water is plentiful and is not valued as a resource. Many Russians think it quite comical if asked to consider the costs of getting that water to them. Likewise, electricity and heating were heavily subsidized and bountiful forests and wildlife are virtually unprotected, rendering the idea of resource conservation absurd.

Some subsidies continue today, but are being progressively reduced. A profound ignorance of the value of goods and services, particularly those based on natural resources, lingers.

Unsurpassed Riches

In 1991, the Kremlin lost 35 percent of its territory to the thirteen newly independent states. No matter. The Russian Federation today remains by far the largest national land territory in the world. Contrary to the common perception of the worthless vast tundra and empty steppe, a large majority of natural resources lies below the same frozen surface.

The wealth of Russia's natural resources indeed is proportional on a world scale to its east-to-west distance over 7,000 miles and eleven time zones. Russia's reserves of total world supplies are estimated to be 25 percent of all known oil reserves, 40 percent of gas reserves, 20 percent of coal reserves, 15 percent of gold reserves and 15 percent of world wood resources. Known reserves include six billion tons of oil, thirty-one trillion cubic meters of natural gas, and 180 billion tons of coal. Russia's natural reserves thus rank first in the world in gas and oil, and second in coal and lumber.

Dependence on Nature

Russia's treasure chest of natural resources is of course an economic blessing that protects against catastrophe while the country sheds its Soviet past. Raw material export earnings help support economic reforms and avoid severe social conflict. Certainly, during times of economic emergency, Russia has sold gold and diamonds on the world market at low prices to get quick cash for feeding the population. Today's hard times permit Russians to overlook the large discount sale of their nation's riches to the West. Resources, many feel, are unlimited.

On the other hand, the apparent growing dependence on raw material sales is a short-term strategy. With riches strewn across the country, there is no pressing need to advance technologically and become an international economic competitor.

Relying on the sale of bits and pieces of the land also fosters another problem. Russia's extraction processes tend to be crude and create excessive pollution. Large-scale ecological damage infects many mining regions and will likely have long-term social consequences. As Russians today confront the statistics of an average lifespan of only fifty-eight years for men and sixty-eight for women, it seems unlikely that in the long term they will remain indifferent to the unhealthy ecological effects resulting from mining.

Russia's economic reliance on the sale of its natural resources is by no means without precedent. During the last decades of the nineteenth century, raw materials were the most important part of Russia's foreign earnings. Coal, lumber, minerals and furs were exported to Western Europe. As a result, many Russian nobles could afford to spend much of the year touring Western Europe. After 1917, the Soviet Union exported raw materials in exchange for the Third World's acceptance of socialist ideology.

The Big Obstacle

A single obstacle hinders efforts to mine Russia's incredible natural wealth—transportation. Distances and remoteness are the most daunting on earth. Russia's unsurpassed riches need to be transported to her ports and railways and it is through the primitive transportation infrastructure that those natural resources must now largely be exported. Oil and gas pipelines from the Soviet period are rusting and the railway is largely in disrepair. Sections of the trans-Siberian railway remain single-track. Businesses which can overcome delivery problems are destined to win large earnings.

Oil

Russia's most relished natural resource today is its oil. Russia and the former Soviet republics have made clear their need for infrastructure investment to extract oil in return for a percentage of profit. No major Western oil company has stayed on the sidelines. Something like oil boom towns have been created on a modest scale in some Northwestern regions. Yet stories circulate about mere laborers earning thousands of dollars per month and lighting cigarettes with ten dollar bills.

But the oil market suffers from terrible turmoil. Each month brings news of Western oil companies which have had to change drastically their investment strategies as new political alliances, bureaucratic reorganization and tax regulations suddenly surface.

The heyday for Western oil companies came in 1990 and 1991. Unscrupulous Russian bureaucrats profited from new political independence and the then huge price differences between the domestic market and world oil prices. Even if they undercut world oil prices by 20 percent during that period, Russian exporters often realized 100 to 200 percent profits above those they received on the domestic market. A big percentage of the oil sale money found its way into the private Western bank accounts of Russian oil managers.

Moscow tried to stop the flight of capital in 1994 by giving only 14 of the previous 38 Russian oil export companies the right to export for hard currency. Export quotas on those 14 "special exporters" were released as of January 1, 1995 in an effort to privatize the industry more fully.

The major risk for Western oil investors in Russia is a legal one. Technological difficulties in the Russian field can be surmounted with proper investment, and Western oil companies have worked in such conditions in Alaska and other parts of the world. At least such difficulties can be studied and problems are predictable.

But the legal realm is largely unstable in Russia—and especially in an industry with such enormous profits. As each of the world's major oil corporations has concluded deals with Russian officials in such (Northwest) regions as Komi and Tyumen of the Russian Federation, each has come to learn months and even years later that former government officials with whom their original contracts were signed have been removed and their government branches eliminated. Original contracts are then declared invalid by the Russian side or at least become irrelevant in practice. The Western partner must start at square one with an entirely new government agency and new set of officials. This same scenario occurs today at an alarmingly regular schedule.

Natural Gas

Natural gas is Russia's second most lucrative export, surpassing in reserves even that of Russia's known oil holdings. Russia indeed uses a large amount of its own natural gas reserves, and exports a large amount to its former socialist brothers in Eastern Europe. Many former Soviet republics depend almost exclusively on Russia's gas supplies, and several have fallen heavily into debt to Russia as a result. Ukraine is the most visible example of an independent former republic whose debt continues to threaten even its independence from Russia. Belarus appears contented to fall largely under Russia's political domain in return for stable energy supplies.

Yet Russia's use of a decade-old pipeline network that runs through now foreign territory in the "near abroad" is equally problematic. Ukraine itself has made it clear to Russia that pipelines to Romania and Bulgaria running through Ukrainian territory may well be subject to increased excise taxes in future. A new pipeline into Poland has received official acceptance from both Russian and Polish sides and is to be completed before the end of the decade. The most critical question of natural gas reserves and sales, as with oil, thus remains one of delivery and transportation to both established and potential buyers.

Other Key Resources

Russia's coal industry was in the throes of domestic labor unrest in early 1995. Given that many of the coal mines are now unprofitable and future miner unemployment inevitable, coal mining will probably hamper the development of this market as a major export earner for Russia in the next few years.

In the same way that miners became the most vocal labor group for economic political changes in 1988 and 1989, so today the large number of 1.5 million workers in the Russian coal industry continues to demand the government's closest political attention. Those miners work in cities where mining supports 90 percent of the local economy. Those areas will be devastated economically when production stops altogether. While foreign investment is severely needed to improve inefficient mining techniques today, decades of wasteful Soviet methods have depleted easily accessible reserves.

Lumber in Russia is estimated to be already in the firm hands of a several multinational lumber consortia, many of them based in Southeastern Asia, and some of them American. Tax and other regulations are continually reviewed by government. In particular, environmental programs financed by the foreign lumber exporters have until now not been required by Russian regulation. Yet those multinational companies already logging in Eastern Siberia have reaped enormous profits with little long-term investment in the area.

Metal and mineral sales to the West must directly confront a volatile world market, and one that Russia single-handedly has been able to affect in the past. In 1992, Russian exporters' efforts to sell as much aluminum as possible in a few months lowered the world price of aluminum by an incredible 40 percent. The sale of other metals, such as platinum and copper, have given only moderate returns within Russia's export market as a whole. Again, the personal profits for certain Russian managers can nevertheless be enormous.

Precious stone and metal trade is minor, but by no means insignificant. A South African diamond consortium feared a dumping of Russian diamonds on the gold market in the fall of 1994, and organized sanctions against Russia if such a dumping occurred. Russia's exported gold is difficult to track, as the vast majority is traded through third-party countries before it is bought in the West. Moscow's own Central Bank gold reserves nonetheless appear to be modest in comparison to those of the United States. Uranium deposits in Russia represent approximately 25 percent of the world's known reserves.

Glossary

Banya   public bath.

Beeznismyeni   "businessmen"; a term often used in a derogatory sense as a synonym for "borderline criminal".

Bookhalter   accountant or bookkeeper.

Chyelnok   "shuttler"; an individual who constantly shuttles back and forth between Russia and a low-cost country with a lot of baggage, usually by car or train, buying in one country and selling in another.

Dacha   country cottage.

Diedovshchyna   brutal hazing rituals which military recruits are often subject to.

Dieta shop   originally intended as a store to sell dietetic food. Today, however, the *Dieta* sells all types of food.

Dyengi   money.

Dyet Maross   "Grandfather Frost"; who brings good children presents on December 31.

Elektrifikatsiya   in the 1920s, Lenin's program to modernize Russia, which included bringing electricity to the vast country.

Glasnost   "openness"; a program launched by Mikhail Gorbachev in the 1980s to encourage a more open society.

Gospadin   "Gentleman"; pre-Revolutionary title of address.

Gospazha "Madam"; pre-Revolutionary title of address.

Inostrantsy "foreigners"; how Russians refer to their foreign guests.

Intelligentsiya traditionally a small social category of well-educated persons, usually free-thinking, politically active and agents of social and political change in Russia.

Iskyat na zhopu prikluchenni "to look for adventures on one's ass"; meaning courting trouble by doing something dangerously stupid and unnecessary.

Krisha literally "roof", a slang word for "protector"; usually a security firm or mafia organization, which will intervene to protect its client.

Kulak "fist"; a derogatory reference to rich peasant farmers with their own land who were said to selfishly hold all their wealth in a tight fist.

Nalog inspektsia office of tax inspection.

Na lyeva "on the left"; to accomplish something in non-official, usually illegal, ways.

Na remont under repair or renovation.

Nomenklatura during Soviet times, a small privileged percent of the population, including high Communist Party officials, top bureaucrats and high-ranking military and their families.

Novie Russkie "New Russians"; young and rich post-communist Russians.

Novy Gode "New Year"; celebrated December 31 and January 1. A holiday at the same level as Christmas in the West.

Parilka steam room.

Perestroika literally "restructuring"; a program launched by Mikhail Gorbachev in the 1980s to restructure Soviet society.

Pokhazuhka "for show"; deception involving cosmetic changes as opposed to substantial change usually to fool foreigners.

Professionalnaya uchilsya a person who has studied to work in a trade, such as a tailor or carpenter.

Propiska a precious document that allows a Russian citizen to reside in a specific city. The propiska system was used to monitor the Soviet population and control mobility.

Remontnik repairperson.

Ruka ruky moiyet "one hand washes the other"; used in an envious and sometimes cynical sense to describe someone's obvious use of personal connections strictly for mutual benefit of the parties involved.

Skritaya reklama "hidden advertising"; an article that appears to be objective but in reality has its content dictated by the person or company commissioning it.

Slavophiles a category of Russians who fiercely push for an all-Slavic way of life and want less foreign influence in Russia.

Somopol a makeshift repair or construction job involving homemade parts.

Spakoistvi "serenity"; during Soviet times, referred to a politically obedient workforce that would ensure a nonrebellious atmosphere on the job.

Stakhanovets workers workers who labored to exceed their norms and join the ranks of the superhuman laborer.

Stolovaya cafeteria.

Svetloye budushcheye "shining future"; a standard piece of communist rhetoric, to which the population supposedly strived.

Svyazi personal connections.

Technikum a technical school that trains students to become mechanics, for example.

Ti the informal "you"; used for friends, children and immediate family.

Torgovyi agyent "trade agent"; similar to commission agents, they represent many companies at once and go store to store attempting to sell for them on commission.

Tovarisch "Comrade"; the common label of address during Soviet times.

Trudavaya knyeshka labor book, which is held by the employer and contains details of a person's work history.

Univermag department store.

Universam grocery store.

Uravnilovka the system of equal pay for the same work regardless of individual effort.

Vodka the national drink of Russia and an endearing national symbol.

V principe "in principle", usually meaning "ideally"; a phrase often used by Russians to mean "Ideally, everything should be all right . . ."

Vui the formal "you".

Vyenik "tree branch", usually from the birch tree, used to whack the skin in the steam room and stimulate circulation while adding scent.

Vzyat s potolka   "to take from the ceiling"; equates with the English "out of thin air".

Zakuski   "snacks".

Zapadniks   a category of Russians in favor of adopting Western ideas and who generally welcome Western influences. They are the opposite of the *Slavyanophil*.

Zoloteya ruki   "golden hands"; this is said about a person who can repair that which others have declared unrepairable.

INDEX

Notes

Notes

Notes

Notes

TITLES OF INTEREST IN
BUSINESS AND INTERNATIONAL BUSINESS

For further information or a current catalog, write:
NTC Business Books
a division of NTC Publishing Group
4255 West Touhy Avenue
Lincolnwood, Illinois 60646–1975